Charlie Peace

For Alison, the love of my life, who will never cease to believe in me;
and for my family, who supported me throughout.
My heartfelt thanks will never be enough to show the gratitude
I owe to each, and every one, of you.

Also, thanks to Trevor Stockbridge, my fellow adventurer and
unofficial chauffeur, and Simon Rodgers, who just wanted
to be mentioned in this book.

Charlie Peace

*Murder, Mayhem and the
Master of Disguise*

Ben W. Johnson

First published in Great Britain in 2016 by
TRUE CRIME
an imprint of
Pen and Sword Books Ltd
47 Church Street
Barnsley
South Yorkshire S70 2AS

ISBN 978 1 47386 298 2

Printed and bound in England
by CPI Group (UK) Ltd, Croydon, CR0 4YY

Typeset in Plantin by
CHIC GRAPHICS

Pen & Sword Books Ltd incorporates the imprints of
Pen & Sword Archaeology, Atlas, Aviation, Battleground, Discovery,
Family History, History, Maritime, Military, Naval, Politics, Railways,
Select, Social History, Transport, True Crime, Claymore Press,
Frontline Books, Leo Cooper, Praetorian Press, Remember When,
Seaforth Publishing and Wharncliffe.

For a complete list of Pen and Sword titles please contact
Pen and Sword Books Limited
47 Church Street, Barnsley, South Yorkshire, S70 2AS, England
E-mail: enquiries@pen-and-sword.co.uk
Website: www.pen-and-sword.co.uk

Contents

Prologue   Hard Times in the Steel City.. 7

Chapter 1   A Devil Born in Angel Court....................................... 15

Chapter 2   Moonlight and Drainpipes.. 24

Chapter 3   The Rogue's Return 34

Chapter 4   Romance and Retribution 43

Chapter 5   Three Irish Brothers 54

Chapter 6   Bullets Fly in Banner Cross 65

Chapter 7   'A Man of Very Bad Character' 74

Chapter 8   One-Armed Jemmy 83

Chapter 9   Bullets Fly in Blackheath... 94

Chapter 10   The First Judgement.. 105

Chapter 11   The 05:15 to Sheffield... 115

Chapter 12   The Second Judgement.. 124

Chapter 13   Prepare for Eternity, Charlie Peace 134

Chapter 14   Mr Marwood's Rope 145

Epilogue..155

Index 158

Prologue:

Hard Times in the Steel City

'If the people of Sheffield could only receive a tenth part of
what their knives sell for by retail in America,
Sheffield might pave its streets with Silver.'
William Cobbett, Politician,
Journalist and Agriculturalist, 1763-1835

heffield is one of the five largest cities in England, yet in the realms of British crime, seems to have been a minor player as a setting for tales of murder and depravity. That isn't to say that this northern metropolis hasn't suffered its share of crime, but many would struggle to name an infamous villain hailing from this thriving city. Fleetingly mentioned in a meagre handful of famous cases, Sheffield was the site of Peter Sutcliffe's last stand, and the destination to which the wife of Reginald Christie would so often disappear, leaving her husband alone to find new forms of degeneracy on each occasion.

Yet, from this industrial region hails one of the most intriguing, and notorious murderers of the nineteenth century. A man who is still talked about by a handful of scholars and historians; yet is perplexingly unknown to most true crime aficionados outside the South Yorkshire area. His wax effigy was once one of the most visited exhibits in Madame Tussaud's Chamber of Horrors, yet his story began to disappear almost as soon as the wax was melted down to create an image of some other terrible, macabre character from the pages of the penny dreadfuls.

The tale itself paints a picture of a physically unusual man with a volatile temper, but with a love for animals, art and music, and who was briefly the most wanted man in Britain. A man who could exhibit traits of both cultural richness and moral bankruptcy almost at the blink of an eye. It is almost a crime itself that the fascinating story of such a villain has been largely allowed to slip, unnoticed and scarcely remembered, from the history books.

To truly know the man, we must get to know his background, and the lifestyle and social factors which led to his rise to grotesque infamy. This is the story of a man who balanced his base acts of cruelty and greed with flashes of criminal genius, and more than his deserved share of good luck. This is a life which is littered with dark twists and turns, and a story which is wastefully slipping away from the urban legend and folklore of not only the nation, but also the history of his home town.

It is in this very town that we begin, but not in our lifetime, or the lifetime of our subject. We must imagine ourselves travelling back to a small patch of land on the banks of a river in Yorkshire.

Sheffield has existed as a settlement ever since its first humble and primitive homes were lovingly built from mud and straw on the banks of the bountiful River Sheaf over a thousand years ago. This was the ideal location for farming, fishing and hunting. It enjoyed everything a community needed to survive in a life as hard and unyielding as the steel which one day would be produced here.

However, despite its natural charms, and unlike some of the other major British cities, Sheffield was a slow developer, and remained a small village until the Norman Conquest. A small castle was built in what is now the thriving city centre, from which the local Saxon inhabitants could be controlled and kept under close observation.

Perhaps there was more to Sheffield than met the eye of its occasional visitors. The building of a castle to govern over such a small community seems such a drastic step by the apparently nervous Normans, that it is reasonable to assume that this was valuable land, and needed to be treated as such.

It is true that the surrounding countryside was a treasure trove of natural resources, and that the sheltered valley surrounded by seven hills made this an ideal outpost in which to settle. But maybe somebody had also dreamt of what this area may one day become? An unbreakable heart of steel and coal; beating in the geographical ribcage of England.

These small settlements slowly began to grow, until the local villages began to rub shoulders with one another, and the villages melted together like molten steel. What began as a single, primitive dwelling had expanded first into a small settlement, then a few small settlements, then a handful of tiny villages, until these villages linked arms and became a town.

It was still a small town; the whole of Norman Sheffield could now nestle comfortably within the boundaries of the modern city centre. Seemingly happy with its new status, and far enough from the more populous towns to bother with all the grandeur and politics of the developing nation, Sheffield continued to grow, but at a rate which suited its humble beginnings.

Some three centuries later, and with the castle reduced to rubble beneath the city centre, it was time for the town to peep out from behind its humble hiding place, and the hard-working residents of this slowly expanding town began to be recognised for their skills, notably in the production of knives.

Another two centuries passed until the Company of Cutlers in Hallamshire was formed to oversee the production of cutlery and weaponry, for which the town was beginning to make its name. Sixteenth century Sheffield collectively slapped itself on the back for being officially the second greatest producer of cutlery in England. Of course, the top prize went to London, as it so often did.

This local talent for producing blades of all sizes and uses was to be the factor that lifted Sheffield from its place as a fairly anonymous town in South Yorkshire, and hoisted it above London as the chief producer of British cutlery. This rise in status was due in no small part to the tireless work of two men. Benjamin Huntsman, who in the 1740s took the process of crucible steel production and raised the standard to beyond the grasp of anywhere else in the world, and his fellow Sheffield resident, Thomas Boulsover, who invented the Sheffield plate, thereby producing the very material that is still in use today, and is unlikely to ever be bettered.

The resulting boom in industry brought labourers and their families from far and wide, and the town was threatening to burst at the seams. This demand for production had become the new, thumping, heartbeat of the swelling town, and with the ever growing population came the inevitable monetary reward.

A good financial standing will always bring power, but very rarely to the lives of the workers, toiling for long hours and in dangerous conditions to provide a meagre existence for their families. This instance was no different. Money had replaced the imposing castle which once stood, glowering over the once fledgling community, offering threat and reward in equal measure, and the metal working industry had been silently crowned as the new ruler and controller of Sheffield.

As in any thriving part of the world, people flocked to Sheffield on the promise of a modest wage, a roof above their heads, and a chance of a comfortable life. They brought with them their loved ones, hoping to place a shabbily shod foot onto the ladder of success.

But what they found were cramped living spaces, dangerous working conditions, and a barrier between rich and poor, which was so strong it could have been tempered from the very steel for which Sheffield was becoming world famous. This was a community of hard men and women, leading hard, and often short, lives. The steelworks had become irreplaceable, and yet the working people were largely disposable.

The heart of steel production lay in the Don Valley, between Sheffield, and its coal producing neighbour, Rotherham. This collaboration of resources is one of the defining factors in the success of the steel working industry in this area. Yet, despite the level of productivity and advances in technology which seemed to improve year upon year, very little was improved upon in respect of the safety of the workers in these huge companies or the conditions in which they were forced to work.

However, in the face of adversity, human nature thrives, and an unspoken, and unbreakable, brotherhood between steel workers ensured that even if the factory owners thought of them as nothing more than numbers in a factory, they would often look after each other, and their families before thinking of their own welfare. Social groups were formed, and a number of sayings and unique expressions, used exclusively by these workers, were born out of the flames and soot of these most dangerous workplaces.

The workers themselves were a multicultural group, mostly made up of native Sheffielders, but with many immigrants from Russia, Poland, Ireland and Italy, and a large influx of labourers from other parts of England; and if rumours are to be believed, it was the southerners amongst the ranks who were eyed with the most suspicion by the native workers. Whatever their background, these men had travelled to South Yorkshire to undertake dangerous and dirty work, and any illusions they may have had about seeking their fortunes in the steel industry were quickly shattered.

At the height of steel production, the skies around Sheffield, especially around the Don Valley, were reported by many sources as being black and filled with flames. This kind of pollution would be unthinkable today, but in this industrial heyday, it was thought of as nothing more than the by-product of toil and productivity. And it was in these conditions, that not only the working men, but their wives and children were raised. Generations lived out their lives beneath this dark, ominous cloud.

This isn't the image of Yorkshire which so many held, and still hold, today. So often imagined as a tranquil place with abundant countryside and an impenetrable dialect, England's largest county has long been referred to as God's Own County by generations of proud Yorkshiremen. But maybe, by the time the nineteenth century cast its industrial reach across the ever dwindling countryside, there was also a hint of the devil roaming within this not so green, and not so pleasant land.

Despite the camaraderie and bluff masculinity of the steelworkers, these over-worked labourers were far from happy. The pay was a pittance, and industrial accidents were commonplace, leading many to be forced into a different kind of lifestyle. A world of insecure properties, dark streets, and a town full of strange economic migrants could only lead to a survival of the fittest mentality for many, and a base and criminal way of life.

This is not to say that Sheffield didn't have its decent folk, working their fingers to the bone and trying to lead an honest life. But crime is usually born out of necessity, and when pockets are empty and mouths need to be fed, there is often a community-wide descent into lawlessness. This was a time of gentility, religion, and a population that literally had the fear of God in them, but righteousness couldn't feed a family, or keep a sick child warm. The only hope of survival was work or crime, and many who couldn't work had to make a difficult and life-changing choice.

This threat of a crime explosion served only to force the rich factory owners and society families to circle their wagons, and the gulf in class between rich and poor imperceptibly widened in the face of danger. The people of Sheffield had become largely divided, with the privileged and entitled creating well-appointed garrisons in the more sought after neighbourhoods, while the poor were left to fight amongst themselves over a few scraps thrown from the tables of the well meaning few.

A brief glimpse of hope was to come with the Electoral Reform Act, 1832, in which Sheffield, like many other towns to become powerful during the Industrial Revolution, was granted representation in the House of Commons. Surely this would lend a voice to the workers, and highlight the dire conditions in which these ordinary and God-fearing souls were forced to exist? And of course the views of those whose back-breaking hard work and tireless toil would be heard in the halls of the mighty?

The Reform Act itself was born out of violence and protest, as in the previous year, when any such representation of places like Sheffield was deemed to be unnecessary, and small riots broke out across the country, many in its industrial heartlands. Centres of industry such as Sheffield, Leeds, Manchester and Birmingham were denied representation in Parliament, whereas the upper class hamlet of Dunwich in Suffolk, with its population of 32 people, was benefiting from having not only one, but two Members of Parliament in Westminster.

In the face of widespread unrest, the holders of power eventually saw sense. A new Act was drafted to allow representation to the larger towns and cities in the industrial north. But it was not to be as promised. The eagerly awaited Reform Act was nothing more than a token gesture, an empty vessel of broken commitments and false hope.

Yes, Sheffield would be represented in the House of Commons, and yes, an elected Member of Parliament would be tasked with ensuring accountability from a distant and blinkered government. But this was to be a Member of Parliament for whom only three percent of the town's population would have the chance, or the right, to vote.

Could this be the spark that would ignite a town in which social injustice and class warfare threatened to explode at any given moment?

The mood of the town simmered with a mix of rage from the downtrodden many, and fear from the represented few. Something had to give, but only when the time was right, as random acts of protest and insubordination could be easily quashed by the, albeit inexperienced, police force. These policemen nervously roamed the streets of the working class areas, with their truncheons grasped tightly and whistles kept a hair's width from their lips. Any act of protest had to be well organised, and had to be in great numbers, in order to achieve the desired effect. The town would be known to the House of Commons one way or another.

Election Day arrived, and authorities were dismayed at the turn out outside the Town Hall. This was more than three percent of the city, and these were certainly not the genteel Lords and businessmen who would be entrusted with the welfare of the town. This was an orchestrated uprising of the working class, largely initiated by the Trade Unions and Social Reform groups. The people had risen, and were marching on *their* Town Hall in order to ensure that *their* opinions were not lost among the pomp and circumstance of this momentous day.

As in the previous year, similar protests were taking place in towns and cities across the nation. Manchester, Liverpool, Leeds, Derby, Nottingham, and any other sizeable town had staged their own version of this spectacular uprising. But, in Sheffield, things were about to turn sour, and the streets were about to be emptied to the sounds of screams and gunshots. Dreams of democracy were to be shattered as the unarmed masses became too loud and too sizeable for the authorities.

The fledgling police force had long since retreated, only to be replaced by the might of the military. Armed with only songs, placards, and a thirst for justice, the protestors suddenly found themselves facing sabres, rifles and pistols. No matter how strong the desire for equality and free speech was, when faced with weaponry and a trained army, there could only be one winner. This was sabres against social injustice, and bullets against brotherly bravado.

So great was the number of people marching through the town centre that those at the front found it difficult to retreat in the face of military intervention, whilst those at the back continued their march towards the Town Hall, the very symbol of their struggle and oppression. The inevitable was to eventually happen, and at the front of the swarming sea of bodies, somebody had given the order to fire.

Chaos ensued as the protestors fled in every direction, and panic took hold of the town for several terrible moments. This was supposed to be a show of unity and collective strength, but ended with many of the participants rounded up and imprisoned or beaten, and six of the protestors never returning home to their loved ones. The unfortunate half dozen had been cut down by the volley of gunfire, their bodies flung to the cobbles, and their best intentions lost forever.

They were to become the forgotten martyrs of a dream which would never become a reality in the lifetimes of those present on that fateful day, or in the lifetimes of their children, or grand-children.[1] The town would become a city before the voices of its occupants would be heard. This whole dreadful day had been a futile attempt to create a better future for the children of the poor. And in a small house, just a stone's throw from the epicentre of the day's terrible events, one such seven-month old child lay, innocently oblivious to the tragedy of the occasion.

Little was his doting mother to know, as she gazed down at her youngest child, that the innocent boy she tenderly nursed was one day to become more famous than the events of this momentous day, and that this certainly would not be the last time her son heard the echoes of gunshots, and the piercing screams of the wounded and terrified.

The family name of the woman and child was Peace, yet in years to come, Charles Frederick would personify the irony of his surname, and bring anything but peace to the family, or to the world.

1   Universal male suffrage was granted in the UK in 1918. Female suffrage was also granted at this time to those aged thirty and over.

Chapter 1

A Devil Born in Angel Court

*'In any case, you must remember, my dearest, that the main
strength of innocence is innocence itself.'*
Fyodor Dostoyevsky, Russian Novelist,
Journalist and Short Story Writer, 1821-1881

John Peace, Charles' father, may be the only man in history who was to lose his leg *before* choosing to become a wild animal tamer. However, despite his strange career choices and regular trips to far and wide places, this devoted father of four young children could certainly not be accused of allowing his family to go hungry.

His early life was typical of a working class boy in the north of England. There was little time for schooling or education; instead, it was expected that as soon as a boy was strong enough to survive manual labour, he was to be thrust into the dangerous world of northern heavy industry, be it the fiery peril of the steelworks, or the dark, dangerous, subterranean world of the nearby collieries.

Although Sheffield is famous for its steelworks, surrounding towns such as Rotherham and Barnsley were home to numerous coalmines. Work was never in short supply if you had the dedication and strength of character to spend long and arduous days in a dark, dangerous pit, seeing very little sunlight, especially in the winter months.

This was a man's world, a place where death and injury were commonplace, yet friendships and camaraderie held these groups of pale and dishevelled workers together through thick and thin. A collier was more than a worker; he was a member of a brotherhood, a fraternity who risked life and limb each day in order to put food onto the tables of their families.

John had been forced underground at an early age, and was already an experienced and hardened collier by the time the youngest of his four children was born. However, in contrast to his bleak and gloomy place of work, John Peace had always shown a spark of adventure, and a love for the more colourful aspects of life - traits which would soon be passed from father to son.

He and his wife, Jane (née Hadlington), the daughter of a naval surgeon, had set up home in Angel Court, central Sheffield, which is now known as Angel Street and is located in the heart of the modern city centre. It was in this modest home that John and Jane doted upon their children, with John being a seemingly fun and fascinating father to the four Peace children.

His love of the arts, especially music, made John a popular man in the area of central Sheffield in which the family lived. Always ready with a joke on his lips and a song in his heart, this was a man who saw beauty in everything, and appreciated the light relief afforded to him by music and theatre, a common trait in those who spent their days working in the cruellest of conditions.

However, life for John, and the entire Peace family was to take an unexpected turn in the wake of tragedy. A terrible accident sustained during a pit collapse at work saw this lively and jovial young man lose a leg to his injuries. Such was the character of John Peace, it would take more than a lost limb to suppress the love of life which he held so dear; but in early Victorian England, it took more than a smile and a cheery song to maintain a family home.

The accident had failed to break the spirit of the Peace family, but certainly threatened to cast the household into a world of poverty and need. The industrial cities were already rife with malnourishment and forgotten families surviving on scraps of food, yet John Peace was a man on whom his family could rely, and he turned his attentions to a unique change of career.

As well as his love of the arts, John Peace was also an animal lover. There was not a local pet or hungry stray which he would not try to befriend or tame, such was his concern as to the well-being of all living things. It was with this in mind that the newly unemployed and disabled Peace decided to take a chance at a career which would encompass his inimitable work ethic, and his love of animals.

The early Victorian period was a heyday for all kinds of travelling shows, since people were travelling further, and exploring deeper than ever before. The public were thirsty for any knowledge of the world they lived in, and the draw of a travelling animal show brought thousands of people to each location.

It was with this in mind that Peace made contact with the owner of one such business (with the help of his wife Jane, who aided her semi-literate husband in writing a letter), asking for employment and boasting of his prowess in taming any animal with which he was to come into contact. To his surprise he was soon to receive a reply, inviting him to join the travelling show, and introducing the respondent as his future employer.

The man who had taken the time to put pen to paper and who was willing to take a chance on a one-legged former collier was already something of a national celebrity owing to the success of his shows, and it was without hesitation that John Peace bid his family farewell and packed his bags to join Wombwell's Travelling Menagerie, vowing to send money at every possible opportunity.

The owner of the menagerie was George Wombwell, a former shoemaker who had begun to make his fortune as a showman after a chance meeting at London Docks, during which he bought two boa constrictors from a sailor returning from a trade visit to South America. The asking price of £75 had been a small fortune to a working man, but after a few weeks of exhibiting his prized possessions around various inns and taverns, his investment had almost paid for itself.

As his profits began to mount, Wombwell became interested in adding new specimens to his show, eagerly awaiting the return of ships from far off places from which he could buy these strange and exotic creatures. By 1810, just six years after purchasing the two snakes, his collection had grown to such a size that he was able to fund, and fill, his own show venue in the Soho area of London.

However, the limitations of a static exhibition soon became apparent to Wombwell, who realised that in order to maximise the profit available to him, his show needed to be seen by as many people as possible, thus the idea of a travelling show was born, and new exhibits, as well as handlers such as John Peace, were picked up along the way.

By the time John Peace had joined the show, the menagerie already boasted a rhino, two elephants and a gorilla, as well as giraffes, leopards, six lions, three tigers, a plethora of monkeys, and several other big cats. Even in today's world, this would have made for an impressive show.

Yet, despite Wombwell's apparent love for all things living, it would seem that his main concern was making money, rather than the desire to care for his animals, since the colder climate of Great Britain saw several of his animal perish within weeks of arrival. Ever the businessman, Wombwell did recoup some of his expenses by selling the cadavers to taxidermists or medical schools.

His questionable activities also stretched into the cruel world of baiting, most noticeably a fight arranged between his lion, Nero, and six bulldogs belonging to an acquaintance. Nero refused to fight, and not willing to lose face or money, Wombwell simply swapped Nero for another lion, by the name of William, who sadly dispatched the six bulldogs in a matter of moments.

However, the leaps made in animal study which were attributed to Wombwell's show were impressive, especially in the case of the aforementioned William, who was the first lion to be bred in Britain, thus proving that our chilly climate *could* sustain exotic creatures from the far corners of the globe.

Despite his great love for his unusual work, John returned to Sheffield just a few years later on the tragic death of his eldest son, also John , who had died after a short battle with tuberculosis. Re-joining his wife, Jane and his remaining children, Peace began to earn a living in the far less glamorous occupation of shoemaking. However, his thirst for adventure had certainly made an impression on one of his surviving offspring.

During her husband's absence, Jane Peace had raised her children to be a credit to the family. They were schooled as comprehensively as possible, and were regular attendees at the local church, and its Sunday school. Although seemingly less adventurous than her husband, Jane Peace was certainly the glue which held the family together, and would remain so for the rest of her life.

Of the three remaining Peace children, Mary Ann, Daniel and Charles, it was the youngest child, 12 year old Charlie, who had become the most noticeable chip off the old block. Deeply saddened by the loss of the younger John Peace, the family found solace in the cheery nature, and happy disposition of this loving and imaginative boy.

Devoted to his mother, and dedicated to his father, Charlie had attended at least two schools in central Sheffield, which would indicate that he had been fortunate enough to benefit from an education which would have been fairly comprehensive for a working class northern child at this time. However, despite his efforts and obvious intellect, young Charlie was not by any means an academic.

His time at school was largely spent on extracurricular activities, such as performing skits and singing songs of his own composition, much to the delight of his many friends. His talents as a musician were noticeable even at an early age, and despite the regular flow of unsatisfactory report cards, his musical talents were nurtured and appreciated by his parents, who glowed with pride when their youngest child picked up one of many instruments and began to play.

Such was his musical talent, especially in playing the violin, that young Charlie was often referred to in local circles as 'the modern Paganini' and regularly performed in church halls and taverns, before passing round a hat in order to boost his family's modest income. The local men were enthralled by his flawless performances, and were often only too keen to throw a few pennies in his direction.

Charlie was, like his father, a natural showman, and spent many hours perfecting basic magic tricks in order to entertain anyone who took the time to watch. His dedication to learning the skills of an entertainer was unquestionable, yet, in the eyes of his school masters, this was a boy who had wasted his intellect and talent on wholly unnecessary and questionable subjects.

In addition to his skills as a showman, Peace was also something of an athlete. Although failing to excel in the more traditional sports which were encouraged during his school years, Charlie was as agile and energetic as a monkey, and would often reduce his friends to gasps of disbelief as he climbed trees and buildings in remarkable time, without an ounce of fear or trepidation.

He was also becoming skilled in creating props to aid his impromptu performances, most notably fashioning a strange cup-like device which he would fasten to his head, before throwing a ball made from heavy shot into the air and effortlessly catching it in the cup. This was a boy with unusual, yet impressive talents, and a sense of adventure which can only be inherited from an unorthodox father like John Peace.

Another trait which had seemingly been passed on from father to son was John's love of animals, and his talents for taming even the wildest of beasts. Many hours were spent between the two, discussing the world of exotic animals, and for once in his life, Charlie was more than happy to be schooled, constantly poring over even the finest details of this fascinating subject.

Like his father, Charlie had a natural affinity with animals, and often took it upon himself to tame the fierce dogs which prowled the neighbourhood and caused his friends to scarper from their barks and growls. It was also a regular occurrence for Charlie to arrive home after school clutching an injured or starving animal, which he would lovingly nurture back to health, before releasing his patient back into the wild.

Had this amiable and intelligent young man been born into a more privileged world, the possibilities for his future would have been endless. However, despite his unique talents, he was still a working class boy from an industrial northern town, and as such, had little choice but to live the life expected of him.

By the tender age of fourteen Charlie's schooldays were behind him, and he followed in the footsteps of the other men in his family by entering the drab and dangerous world of manual labour. This was simply the way of the world in Victorian Sheffield, yet not one complaint was made by this talented boy, who, like his father, worked diligently, and dreamed of adventure.

However, it was not long into his career as a steelworker in the Millsand Rolling Mill that the curse which had struck his father was also passed on to Charlie. He was still in his first year as a labourer when tragedy struck. Like his father some years before, young Charlie was to be on the receiving end of a tragic accident in the workplace.

In a world where scars and missing fingers were commonplace, it was unsurprising that a young employee would eventually fall victim to the glowing steel which was hoisted around the workplace with little regard for human safety. Yet it was the severity of the injury which came as a shock to John and Jane Peace, who rushed to the hospital to see their gravely injured youngest son.

A piece of molten steel had entered Charlie's leg below the knee, penetrating the limb like a glowing knife through butter. So severe was the injury that it was widely believed by the doctors who attended his bedside that this unfortunate young man would, sooner or later, have to prepare himself for the same fate which had befallen his father, the tragic loss of a leg.

Yet, in part due to the diligence of the doctors and also in part due to the strength of character abundant in Charlie Peace, his injured leg was not to be amputated; instead, months of painful treatment and a slow rehabilitation enabled this once-athletic young man to walk again, but not before enduring the kind of pain and torment which would have reduced an older and stronger man to tears.

By the time he left the infirmary, Charlie had been a resident there for over eighteen months, receiving daily visits from his loving family and friends, glad of the attention and the opportunity to try out his latest skit or magic trick. He may have been physically impaired, but, like his father, young Charlie would not allow such a setback to hamper his unbreakable spirit.

Although able to rise to his feet and walk a few paces, it was obvious to anyone who spent time assisting him in his rehabilitation that Charlie would never regain full use of his leg. He would spend the rest of his life cursed with a pronounced limp and constant aches and pains. Yet, such was the character of this indomitable young man that he thanked his lucky stars each day that he was still fortunate enough to have kept his injured leg.

Now back on his feet and having returned home to Angel Court, the next obstacle to overcome was the inability to work, and limited mobility, which had been a result of the accident. No employer would hire a crippled novice, especially in the factories and mines which had previously provided Charlie's only realistic chances of a career.

Like his father, Charlie had been unceremoniously forgotten by the very workplace which had robbed him of his health and mobility and, also like his father, he had received nothing in compensation for the injury he had sustained. This was a world where a man knew the dangers of his trade, and accepted them as part of the job. No duty of care was required, and certainly no sense of loyalty to an injured employee existed.

For the first time in his life, Charlie Peace became victim to a sense of hopelessness, and began to brood upon his predicament. The change in him was noticeable; gone was the happy-go-lucky young man whose limits knew no bounds; instead, in his place was a young man who had too much time on his hands to dwell upon the cruel blow which had been inflicted upon him.

Despite his anguish, and in duty to his family, Charlie would still pick up his violin and entertain the drinkers in the local taverns, gladly accepting the coins thrown into his hat at the end of each performance. Yet, this was nothing more than a pittance to offer to his parents, and he was only too aware that a greater income must be found.

Whilst still convalescing, a further blow was dealt to Charlie and his family, as his beloved father was taken ill and died just a short time later. It was John's income as a shoemaker which had provided the food on the table of the Peace family, and without this, the future began to look increasingly bleak.

Yet it wasn't the lack of income which affected young Charlie so deeply. It was the loss of his beloved father, a man who had been the source of love, knowledge and fatherly pride to his youngest son throughout his life, gifts which had been gladly appreciated by a young boy who had dreamed of being like his father and living a life full of hope and adventure.

The entire family were devastated, but none more so than Charlie, who slipped into a deep depression, becoming withdrawn and sombre. Not only had he lost the man whom he had loved more than anyone in the world, he also had a duty to provide for his family. He found himself to be nothing more than a crippled musician with little chance of employment, and the weight of providing for the family could not be solely borne by his elder brother, Daniel.

For the first time in his life, Charlie became unruly, staying out until the early hours of the morning and often returning with cuts and bruises after picking a fight in the local tavern. This wasn't the Charlie Peace that his family and friends knew and loved. He was becoming a darker and more threatening individual, turning away from those who sought to help him through his black moods.

The change in her youngest son alarmed Jane Peace, who had seen him change from being a vivacious and happy child into an angry and volatile young man in the space of just a few months. Yet little did she know the future which awaited her beloved Charlie and the lengths to which he would go in order to raise income for the family, and for his own, newly developed vices.

Chapter 2

Moonlight and Drainpipes

'If criminals would always schedule their movements like
railway trains, it would certainly be more convenient for all of us.'
Arthur Conan Doyle, British Author, 1859-1930

The deterioration of his cheery soul and pleasant character had caused much concern to those who loved and cared for Charlie Peace, so much so, that his doting mother, Jane, saw fit to remove herself and her troubled son to Hull in early 1851. Staying with John Greer, a family friend, Jane and Charlie were listed there on the 1851 census.

John Greer had a son, James, who was the same age as Charlie, and the two are believed to have immediately struck up a friendship during this extended stay. However, with her other children, Mary Ann and Daniel, having remained in Sheffield, it was only a matter of time before it was necessary for mother and son to return home.

During these few weeks, Charlie had developed an affinity for Hull, and the family with whom he had stayed. There was always money to be made at the estuary docks, whether by legitimate labour, or the odd act of pilfering, an activity which seems to have been an unwelcome addition to the character of young Charlie by this time.

Having reached his eighteenth birthday before embarking on this trip with his mother, Charlie was now a man in the eyes of the law, and it was this coming of age which spurred the young man into a desperate realisation that he had to find a source of income to see him through his life. Yet, unable to work, and with the first green shoots of criminality rising to the surface, it would seem that the die had already been cast as to Peace's future career.

Upon returning to Sheffield, Peace's habitual pilfering had developed into something more sinister. He had taken to being what was referred to as a *'street roller'*, an individual who would stalk the streets looking for the opportunity to relieve an unwitting passer-by of their possessions, whether by use of clever distraction, or a more overt physical threat.

Although never officially documented, owing to Peace's success in avoiding prosecution, it is believed that the first serious criminal act committed by this limping young urchin was the theft of a gold pocket watch from an unsuspecting elderly man, just a few streets away from his home in central Sheffield.

Having made his getaway with the item, which was immediately sold to a pawnbroker in exchange for a handful of coins, there can be no doubt that Peace had hit upon his much needed method of making money. If he could not be employed to work for a living, he would put food on the table by any means possible; after all, the world had yet to do himself and his long-suffering family a favour or two.

However, this particular method of theft was not suited to a young man like Charlie Peace; he was already instantly recognisable to anyone in the local area, being small for his age and with a pronounced limp, which could not be disguised when hurriedly fleeing the scene of a daring street robbery. Peace would have to play to his talents, something which came naturally to a man of his inventive character.

On 26 October 1851, at just nineteen years of age, Peace finally plucked up the courage to commit a crime more suited to a man of his unique talents, and used his natural athleticism to scale the porch of a nearby home before forcing open an upstairs window. This nocturnal activity had come naturally to Peace, and with a bag full of ill-gotten gains, he quietly made his way home through the dark streets, already plotting his next crime.

Things didn't quite go to plan, however, with the lone female owner of the property returning home and finding her valuables missing and immediately summoning the police. A list of the missing items was quickly produced, and circulated to every pawnbroker and policeman in the area, something for which the naive young burglar had failed to plan.

It wasn't long before word got around that Charlie Peace was attempting to sell some valuable items of jewellery, something which was brought to the attention of the local police by a conscientious neighbour. This was a grave mistake on the part of the debutant burglar, and immediately resulted in serious consequences for Peace.

CHARLIE PEACE

Upon searching the family home, the police had no trouble in identifying the stolen objects which had been stashed away in an upstairs bedroom, and Peace was immediately arrested and brought before the magistrate. This had been a terrible start to his planned new career, and punishment could not be avoided in these circumstances.

Owing to his tender age and disability, the magistrate took a lenient approach to sentencing the young man who appeared in the dock before him, sending Peace to prison for one month, no doubt believing that the effects of a stay in prison would shock this fledgling burglar into seeing the error of his criminal ways.

However, upon reaching the end of his short sentence, Peace had not changed his ways; in fact, he had used the time afforded to him in prison to dwell upon his basic errors, vowing that he would be much more careful in future. No longer would he risk his freedom by chasing a few pounds gained from opportunistic crimes, his future would depend on planning and professionalism.

With this in mind, and having made his apologies to his mortified mother for bringing shame upon the family, Peace bided his time considering appropriate premises to target. Passing his night time walks around Sheffield off as a need to be out in the open after his incarceration, he watched every window, and made reams of mental notes as to the comings and goings of the unsuspecting occupants.

The next couple of years saw Peace making ends meet through a number of successful burglaries, always taking care to keep the number of items stolen down to a minimum to aid him in his getaway. His methods were now more measured and considered, yet as most habitual criminals do, he spent every waking hour pondering a huge haul, knowing that he possessed the skills to take his career to the next level.

Despite the anger of his mother which had been apparent during his first prosecution, it would appear that, by this point, at least one family member was complicit with Peace and his crimes, as, rather than storing his haul at the family home, he now used the home of his elder sister to stash the stolen goods.

His relationship with Mary Ann had always been a close one, as being his elder sister, she would regularly step into a more maternal role during his upbringing, something which was appreciated by Charlie. He would reciprocate at any possible occasion, especially when it came to dealing with the violent and abusive man to which Mary Ann had found herself married.

Despite being ready to accept a share of the illegally acquired gains of Peace's crimes in return for storing items at his home, the relationship between Mary Ann's husband, Mr Neil, and her younger brother was volatile to say the least. On several occasions, Charlie had been forced to step in during heated rows between husband and wife, and had regularly delivered a violent reprisal after his sister had been struck by her husband.

One such occasion, which has become almost legendary in the story of Charlie Peace, arose when Peace attended the house after finding his sister with a blackened eye, only for Neil to set his pet bulldog upon the livid young man who had dashed across town to avenge the treatment of his beloved sibling.

Swiftly making a grab for the dog before it sank its teeth into his flesh, Peace had grasped the animal by the jaw, and delivered a punch so powerful that the bulldog was rendered unconscious, leaving him to inflict a similar punishment on Neil, who was quickly retreating into the house. For an animal lover like Peace, this must have been a regrettable occurrence, something which undoubtedly fuelled the ferocious beating he delivered upon his brother-in-law.

This family arrangement for storing the stolen goods came to an abrupt end in 1854, when a stash of misappropriated property was discovered by the police. One can only surmise as to the source of this information, but it is worth noting that the only party to escape punishment was Peace's despised brother-in-law, who even watched as his wife appeared in the dock as part of this investigation.

Having already been convicted of burglary three years earlier, there was to be no leniency shown towards Peace on this occasion, and he was sentenced to four years hard labour in Doncaster prison. This time he would certainly have enough time on his hands to brood upon the circumstances which saw him imprisoned for a second time.

Although furious at his current predicament, Peace was more upset to hear that his sister had been incarcerated as a result of his crimes along with a female friend who had also assisted in the storage of the goods. Both women were sentenced to six months imprisonment, and Peace vowed that he would take more care to protect his family when the time came for him to be released.

The four years of imprisonment did nothing to dampen the criminal appetites of Peace, as during his lengthy sentence he spent his days in conversation with older and more experienced criminals, taking from them advice and tips on how to avoid the law. However, the fact that these men were also behind bars should perhaps have warned Peace as to the merits of their advice.

During his time in Doncaster prison, Peace had been the model prisoner, courteous and well-behaved, and therefore was granted parole in the third year of his sentence. The years had already started to be unkind to the young prisoner, and upon the time of his release, the twenty-five year old convict could have easily passed for a gnarled man in his forties.

With no job to go to, or money to feed himself, it was no surprise that Peace immediately returned to his criminal ways, although this time he decided to make one important change to his methods - he would find himself a partner in crime with whom to ply his dishonest trade.

Unfortunately, the name of this accomplice has been lost to the annals of time, but it is suggested that the man with whom Peace plotted his future burglaries was an acquaintance from his time spent in Doncaster prison. However, in this case, two heads were certainly not better than one, and Peace was to find this latest spell of freedom to be relatively short-lived.

Knowing that any further prosecutions would bring increasingly serious punishments, Peace came to the conclusion that escape from the scene of his crimes was more important than ever, and consequently furnished himself with a revolver in order to scare away any policeman or home owner who threatened to stand in his way.

This was a huge risk, as not only would the possession of a revolver lengthen any sentence he would receive in the future, it might also culminate in the need to fire the deadly weapon, something which, despite his criminal appetites, Peace had no intention of doing. However, circumstances would soon dictate that arming himself against capture was a grave mistake.

Another amendment to Peace's modus operandi was to move his criminal activities away from his own doorstep. Fearful of bringing the police to the door of his family home once again, the two men chose Manchester as the location for their next jaunt into criminality, packing a horse and cart and making the relatively short journey west, before finding cheap lodgings from which to operate.

Having settled into their lodgings, Peace and his accomplice spent many hours walking around the local area under the pretence of being travelling labourers in search of work. This time there could be no mistakes; they would do their intended work before heading back to the relative safety of South Yorkshire, their pockets bulging with the proceeds of a crime which could not be traced back to them.

The two men took their time selecting a house suitable for their requirements, noting the available access points and daily schedules of the occupants. Peace was to be the one who would enter the property, with his accomplice keeping a close watch on the surrounding area, ready to alert his colleague to any advancing threat.

Still blessed with his childhood agility, Peace had become something of a *'portico burglar'* during his formative years of crime, having mastered the art of climbing onto the porch of a house and entering through an upstairs window in order to conceal his presence on the premises. Within seconds of reaching the intended house, he could easily slip through a window twenty feet above the ground.

The initial burglary was a great success for Peace and his accomplice, with the two men rapidly leaving the scene with a large haul of expensive items. However, with nowhere to store the goods since the arrest and imprisonment of his sister, the two burglars made the decision to hide the haul amongst a copse of trees in the nearby countryside.

Unfortunately, the goods were quickly discovered and reported to the Lancashire police, who decided to leave the stolen goods *in situ*, and lay a trap for the guilty parties. All that was required was to keep watch on the area from a distance, and wait for the burglars to return for the proceeds of their crime.

The police did not have to wait for long, as the next day two men began to make their way towards the copse, one of them limping across the fields while furtively surveying the surrounding area. However, the police were well-concealed behind a nearby wall, and had only moments to wait before pouncing upon their prey.

As soon as the two men began to pack the goods into a sack, a group of police constables began to descend upon them from all directions, blocking any possible escape route. This called for decisive action, and for the first time in his criminal career, Charlie Peace was forced to raise his revolver in sheer desperation.

Pointing the gun at the nearest policeman, Peace barked at the oncoming lawmen that he would not hesitate to shoot, but was, thankfully, tackled from behind by another of the constables who had appeared on the scene. Pinned to the ground by an ever-increasing number of uniformed arms, this was to be the last taste of freedom that Charlie Peace would experience for quite some time.

This latest loss of liberty was particularly damaging to Peace, as not only had he recruited a partner in crime during his freedom, he had also found himself a soulmate and lover, in the form of Hannah Haines, a young widow with an infant son, William. For the first time in his life Peace had allowed romance to get the better of him, yet here he was, robbed of his freedom for the third time.

Sentenced to a further six years behind bars, most of which was spent in the notorious Strangeways prison, and dismayed at the premature ending of his courtship with Hannah, Peace spent much of his time writing letters to the object of his affection, and was distraught to hear, just weeks into his sentence, that Hannah was with child. Charlie Peace was about to become a father, but would be unable to take his place at the head of his own household for another six years.

The child, a daughter named Jane after his beloved mother, was raised single-handedly by Hannah until Peace was finally released from prison. This should have been the ultimate warning to the absent father to mend his ways, but, sadly, the talons of crime had buried themselves too deep into the flesh of this wretched villain, and the precious gift of freedom was soon to be discarded once again.

Upon his latest release into society, Peace had wasted no time in setting up home with his wife, stepson and daughter, and within weeks of being reunited with his long-suffering and patient lover the two were married in a small ceremony in nearby Rotherham. Life was looking up for Charlie Peace.

Two years passed without any further incident, as Peace made a conscious decision to curb his more adventurous ideas. He still, however, continued to provide for his family by illegal means, but had learned to take no unnecessary risks which would jeopardise the freedom to be with his family.

The only misfortune to befall Peace during this period of freedom was entirely self-inflicted, as the unwise decision to carry a revolver once again came back to haunt him. Failing to ensure that the safety catch had been engaged on his trusty revolver, the unlucky burglar managed to shoot off two of his own fingers whilst reaching into the pocket of his overcoat.

For a man used to physical pain, and already cursed with physical deformity, the loss of two digits did little to squash the adventurous spirit, although any future comparisons between him and Paganini would be unlikely, as playing the violin to his previous standards would be almost impossible.

However, a man as inventive as Charles Frederick Peace could always find the solution to a problem, so he altered his trusty fiddle and day and night practised holding the bow with his mutilated hand. Before long, he was once again entertaining the drinkers at his local tavern, though admittedly with slightly less panache than before.

Having slipped back into society and finding himself appreciated by his friends and adored by his family, it would be unthinkable for a man in Peace's situation to risk everything on a foolhardy whim, yet such a whim was about to take him, and at the worst possible time for the newly reunited family.

Contrary to his situation at the birth of his daughter, Peace was a free man when his son, John Charles (named after his late father) entered the world. Unfortunately, this habitual criminal was to miss out on seeing another child grow up, all thanks to an unforgivable and wholly out of character error of judgement.

Peace himself admitted to being 'fuddled with whiskey' when he found himself in the familiar surroundings of police custody. Having been so careful to cover his tracks and select *safe* premises to burgle, this costly error was uncharacteristic, but spoke volumes of a man for whom crime ran in the blood. Not even the domestic bliss afforded to him by his wife and children could direct Charlie Peace onto the straight and narrow.

The burglary for which he had been apprehended had been a farce from beginning to end, with the drunken Peace clattering noisily onto the porch of a property, before crashing through an empty bedroom with enough bumps and thuds to wake the dead. This was one of the easiest arrests the police would ever make, with Peace being spotted entering the premises, and grabbed immediately as he emerged from the grounds of the house clutching a sack of valuables.

As the number of Peace's arrests escalated, so did the sentences handed out to him, and this time, the punishment was a harsh eight years of penal servitude. The crime itself had been less serious than his previous punishable offences, but after years of trying to deliver warnings to their wayward prisoner, the authorities had simply had enough of this habitual thief.

This time, Peace's new home would not be Doncaster prison; he was, instead, remanded in the much tougher Wakefield prison for the majority of his sentence. Visiting privileges were strict, and the regime was much more rigorous than any he had previously experienced. However, it was not to be the eight years of hard labour which would hit Peace the hardest; it was the consequences of his absence from the family.

Peace had already missed the formative years of his daughter's life, and was now suffering the same punishment in regards to his infant son. However, the hardest blow was received just less than a year before he was due to be released, when his young son, John Charles, died aged six after a series of illnesses, meaning that Peace had missed out on the vast majority of his child's short life.

Peace blamed himself for the untimely death of his son, reasoning that if he had been in his rightful place at home, he would have been in a position to raise funds for the best treatment available for young John Charles. However, owing to his extensive stays at Her Majesty's Pleasure, an early release had not been an option for this dangerous and prolific criminal.

A further blow came shortly after, when Peace was informed of his beloved sister's untimely passing (believed to be as a result of cancer). This was a man who had already lost more loved ones than one could bear to imagine, and, being kept firmly under lock and key, all he could do was spend long hours reflecting on his misfortune,

The guilt and sadness were almost unbearable to Peace, who brooded in his cell, vowing to make amends with the remaining members of his family. Hannah, Jane, and his beloved stepson Willie needed him, and he would stop at nothing to ensure that he would be able to provide for them again.

One way or another, he swore that would never find himself behind bars again. He had lost too much time with his family to even comprehend spending even one unnecessary moment away from them in the future. He had just under a year left to serve, and to make waves with such a short time remaining would be a foolish and reckless decision.

Chapter 3

The Rogue's Return

*'A fish might more easily live on the apex of a rock than a man
accustomed to crime live a life of virtue.'*
William Beckford, British Novelist, 1760-1844

Charlie Peace had spent almost half of his life imprisoned, yet the toll of prison life was still to weary the determined and stubborn heart which he wore with pride on his sleeve. However, the physical effects of over eighteen years behind bars had caused the prisoner to look much older than his years.

Gnarled, stooping and balding, Peace could easily have passed for a man in his sixties by the time he reached his fortieth birthday. Yet the allure of his young family who counted the days until his release acted as a daily reminder that he still had life left to live, and live it he certainly would. The lure of the outside world was stronger now than at any time during his previous incarceration.

With just eleven months left to bide his time behind the walls of Wakefield prison, the recently bereaved father could contain himself no longer. He had to see his family, and the thought of missing another year of family life was too unbearable to consider. Completely aware of how foolish his plans were for a man with less than a year left to serve, Peace began to plot his escape. He would regain his freedom on his own terms.

Having been a model prisoner for the last seven years, Peace was a trusted inmate, and consequently was allowed to work as a repairman within the gaol. With access to tools and the privilege of being able to move freely around the prison, the temptation of escape had long been present.

Having painstakingly created a saw from off-cuts of tin found in the prison workshop, Peace managed to smuggle a small ladder into his cell one night. Wholly aware of his surroundings, this ingenious inmate knew that there was an escape route just inches above the ceiling of his cell, from where a man of his athleticism could traverse the high walls and find a safe place to drop to safety.

With this in mind, he began to saw through the wooden ceiling, taking care to use his bedclothes to muffle the sound of his progress. Hour by hour, Peace worked tirelessly to create a hole big enough for him to squeeze his diminutive frame through, and before first light he had achieved his goal.

However, having completed the difficult part of his task, it would appear that the lure of freedom had resulted in a bout of over-excitement, as before climbing the ladder to hoist himself through the aperture he had so tirelessly created, the wild-eyed Peace failed to wait for the warders to safely pass his cell during their rounds.

It was a remarkable coincidence that one such warder chose exactly this moment to peer into the cell of the man who had been previously trusted to carry tools and move around the prison. It was with a sense of disbelief that the puzzled warder opened the door hatch just in time to see a trailing foot disappear through the ceiling of the cell.

Immediately unlocking the door and rushing to apprehend the disappearing prisoner, the warder burst into the small room and scaled the ladder with the intention of capturing the escaping inmate. However, as in his criminal career, Peace's slight build and athleticism had once again come to his aid, as the warder was unable to force his own body through the small hole above him.

The alarm was raised, and all available guards were tasked with finding Peace and returning him to the wing. However, Peace had needed only a small head start, and found himself carefully traversing a high wall, watching with fascination as the guards and searchlights frantically sought out their target.

Having successfully negotiated the walls, Peace found himself reaching the edge of the sprawling complex, where he lowered himself into the grounds of the governor's house. This was the last place they would expect to find an escaped convict, but was also a place where he might be able to furnish himself with a disguise.

Finding the house empty, as the governor had been summoned as soon as the alarm had sounded, Peace was able to find some clothes into which he hurriedly changed. However, escaping the house would be a far more difficult task than first imagined, as every guard in the prison was now milling around the grounds, looking for any sign of movement.

For almost two hours Peace hid himself in the governor's bedroom wardrobe, waiting for any opportunity to slip away unnoticed. Unfortunately, no such opportunity arose, and as the guards finally entered the house and made their way to the bedroom, Peace knew that the game was up; there was to be no early freedom for this inmate.

Although his luck had run out during his extended stay in the governor's wardrobe, the attempted escapee was lucky enough to avoid any severe reprisals following his nocturnal adventures. He was transferred to three more prisons during his last year, and his privileges permanently removed, yet no additional time was added onto his sentence, a blessing which the homesick Peace no doubt appreciated.

By the time Peace's eight year sentence had ended, he had endured Yorkshire's toughest prison, almost escaped from his cell, and spent time in Millbank, Chatham, and even Gibraltar. Yet still he was to emerge into the unfamiliar daylight with a wide grin upon his weathered face when his time was up. It was time to live life again, and nobody would take away his freedom while he still possessed even an ounce of his famous determination.

Upon rejoining his family in Sheffield, Peace relocated his loved ones to a new home in the centre of the city. It was to be in this new family home that he planned to make a genuine attempt at family life and, for the time being at least, put his criminal ways behind him in favour of living an honest and hardworking life.

Still haunted by the death of John Charles, Peace's first act as a free man was to present his wife with a lovingly created funeral card in memory of his tragically deceased son, which bore a verse of his own writing:

'Farewell my dear son, by all us beloved, thou art gone to dwell in the mansions above. In the bosom of Jesus who sits on the throne, thou art anxiously waiting to welcome us home.'

Determined to make an honest living for the first time in his adult life, Peace used his skills as a craftsman to set himself up in business as a self-employed picture framer. No longer would his family be ashamed to mention their father; Charlie Peace's future belonged to his devoted wife, Hannah, and to Willie and Jane, the rapidly growing children who had missed their father so acutely during their troubled childhood.

The first step in ensuring a better life for his children was to encourage them to attend the local church on a regular basis. This, Peace believed, would eventually deliver them from the sins of their father, ensuring some kind of salvation for the two youngsters who had been unfortunate enough to have to endure the very worst start in life.

However, Peace himself, although in dire need of salvation, was never to attend the church or Sunday school with Jane and Willie, reasoning that his agnostic beliefs would hinder the spiritual development of the children. Instead, their doting mother, Hannah, took great delight in accompanying the two to services and classes, no doubt thankful of a welcome degree of normality in their lives.

It wasn't that Peace didn't believe in God, he certainly did, and knew the error of his ways more than anyone. But when pressed upon the subject of religion during his long conversations with friends in the local inn, Peace would reply 'I believe in God, and I believe in the devil, but I'm not afraid of either of them.'

Peace was an advocate of self-belief, and was only too aware that the only person who could repair his damaged soul was himself. He was a man who could not be tamed by outside influences, only he could be the judge of his actions and their consequences, and to do this, he must devote the rest of his life to the people who had stuck by him during his darkest hours.

Instead of offering his soul to the church, Peace spent every waking hour striving to become the man he could have been. The first step along this difficult path was to rekindle his love for music. A cheery musical score was more important to him than any passage of the Bible, and a jaunty (and often risqué) ditty was more sacred to him than any hymn.

To supplement his modest earnings as a picture framer (albeit an extremely talented and diligent one), he once again found joy in performing his impromptu one-man shows around the local inns and taverns. His talent and showmanship meant that he would always return home with a pocketful of coins at the end of each evening, minus those which he had passed over the counter to pay for his beer and whiskey.

He would also perform for his family at the drop of a hat, encouraging his children to sing along with him, and gently teaching them the techniques of each instrument in his repertoire. The two children, especially Willie, the stepson whom Peace loved as if he were his own, found great delight in joining their father for a makeshift recital in the parlour. These were the moments which Peace had longed for during his many years under lock and key.

The passion Peace held for animals of all kinds was also to be rekindled, as he took every opportunity to take into his care a wide variety of pets. Whether taking in strays, or buying rare specimens from acquaintances, within months of his release the family house was filled with life of all kinds.

The parlour was festooned with bird cages, all containing colourful and exotic breeds, their unique calls echoing around the house like the sounds heard in some far away tropical rain forest. Outside in the yard were a number of cages and hutches, housing rabbits and ferrets, while a number of dogs and cats prowled the family home, fighting for attention amidst the backdrop of this suburban zoo.

The animals and impromptu musical recitals made the Peace house a popular attraction within the district, and each day the children would arrive home with excited friends in tow, desperate to catch a glimpse of the collection of animals, and eager to be treated to a song and a handful of sweets by the fascinating Mr Peace.

Jane and Willie were happier than ever; this was the kind of upbringing which had been denied them by Peace's failed criminal escapades. They had an army of friends, and a home life which would be the envy of any working class child. Life for the Peace family was good, and each night Hannah, Jane and Willie prayed that it would remain so.

However, whether Hannah Peace simply misjudged the amount of money which could be made by a picture framer and part-time musician, or whether she had simply chosen to bury her head in the sand, she began to notice that the new additions to the household, be it a rare animal or a new musical instrument, were becoming more and more extravagant as each week passed.

Her husband had always been the kind of man who would make his own entertainment in life, spending many hours crafting instruments from pieces of scrap metal and off-cuts of wood, yet these homemade creations now seemed to have been cast aside, replaced by instruments whose obvious craftsmanship would suggest that they were out of reach for the pockets of a self-employed working man like Charlie Peace.

The money brought home by Peace at the end of each day had also increased, even to the point where the family, who had always been respectably but modestly attired, could now afford more expensive clothes. Yet still Hannah Peace did not pry into her husband's affairs; she simply accepted the gifts he showered her with, and hoped that there would be no further trouble around the corner.

As the contents of the house became more luxurious, and the food on the table became more plentiful, it is reasonable to infer that the nervously grateful Hannah thanked her lucky stars each night her husband returned, and each day that went by without a heavy knock on their front door.

Peace would simply pass these gifts off as being the result of a good week at work, but was only too aware that his wife had become suspicious of his new found wealth. Yet, as each day passed, the family unit remained unthreatened, and the expensive contents of their home remained unchallenged. Perhaps her husband was genuinely making honest money for the first time in their marriage?

Had Hannah ever checked on her husband's whereabouts on the evenings in which he was supposedly visiting the tavern to play his violin and spend time with his large group of friends, she would have spotted that something was amiss, as very rarely was her husband actually in the tavern these days.

He was also making regular trips to other towns and cities, supposedly 'on business', yet it would seem unlikely that the demand for a picture framer would necessitate calling in a man from a neighbouring county in order to smarten up a family portrait or measure the dimensions of a watercolour before making it presentable.

In addition, had this trusting and loyal wife ever taken a peek inside her husband's battered and worn violin case before he left for the evening at the tavern, she would have found that the contents were not innocent instruments for making music - they were sinister instruments for forcing entry to the homes of the wealthy and privileged.

Yet the good life went on in the Peace household, and as the children reached maturity, they could now dream of a future which did not consist of poverty and unhappiness. Their father had been true to his word when he had promised to provide for and care for each and every one of the family. Unfortunately, at least one of his other vows, unbeknown to them, had been broken within weeks of his release.

As Hannah Peace continued to hope that their luck would hold out, and her wayward husband would not be forcefully taken from the family again, her husband knew only too well that luck was not a factor with which he was now concerned. All that mattered to Charlie Peace was giving his children the best life possible, and he now had the ways and means of doing so.

During his long stays in prison, Peace had become hardened to the threat of arrest, developing a hatred of and complete disregard for the police who had so often been his sworn enemy. He considered the local constables to be incompetent and bungling imbeciles, and prided himself that he was ten times smarter than an entire constabulary.

Having been arrested at least four times for burglary, one would consider Peace's view of the police as incompetent to be unwise, yet he was only too aware that each time he had been caught it had been of his own making. *He* had been the factor that had landed him in prison, not the crimes he committed.

The undeniable truth was that during his time behind bars, this irrepressible villain had had years and years of opportunity to review his past errors, and take advice from the kindred souls who shared his cells over the long and arduous years. To coin a phrase, the brotherhood of burglars really had been as thick as thieves.

Of course there was always the small possibility that a huge slice of luck would be on the side of the police, but by this point, Peace was a man who believed in percentages, and having honed his skills to a standard which he believed was good enough to avoid capture under the majority of circumstances, he was prepared to play the odds in search of wealth and opportunity.

Since the unfortunate arrest of his recently deceased sister, and the unwise decision to recruit a partner in crime for his escapade into Lancashire, Peace had learned that the way forward was not to trust another living soul. He had learned that his only true allies were time and distance, a formula which had served him well during his latest spell of freedom.

Time was crucial, in that he would never, from this time forward, enter premises without being one hundred percent sure that there was no danger to himself or his freedom. If this involved hours of covert surveillance, so be it. A few hours of tedious waiting in the cold was infinitely more favourable than a few years of waiting in a cell.

Peace had also expanded his professional boundaries to the point that he now favoured performing his break-ins as far away from Sheffield as he could travel. Neighbouring towns such as Rotherham, Doncaster and Barnsley all fell victim to his crimes, as did further towns and cities such as Chesterfield, Nottingham, Leeds and Manchester.

Not only were his nocturnal sojourns relocated away from Sheffield, he also took the 'belt and braces' approach of ensuring that his illicit haul never crossed the boundary into his hometown. Instead, he would select another town, far away from wherever he had staged the burglary, before being satisfied that he could safely, and anonymously, dispose of his booty at a pawnbroker's.

For example, having successfully observed, studied, and subsequently burgled a house in Manchester, his next port of call could have been Nottingham, where the local police would not be on the lookout for the goods, or for a man of his description. It was almost foolproof; a few hours of uncomfortable travel by horse and cart were worth every moment of his freedom.

The amendments which Peace had made to his methods had been successful in aiding his desire to remain safe and free from harassment by the police, yet the majority of his success could still be attributed to the natural skills which had been with him since his first tentative steps into criminal life all those eventful years ago.

He had lost none of his natural athleticism to the ravages of time; he was still more than able to scale a wall within seconds, before contorting his slight frame to fit through seemingly the smallest apertures. He had become the kind of criminal of which legends are created. He was a superb cat burglar, and prided himself on being the best thief in the country.

CHARLIE PEACE

The months of freedom became years, and still no reprisals were experienced by Peace or his family, who by this point had outgrown their small home in central Sheffield. It was time for a move; the Peace family deserved a home to be proud of, and Charlie was only too glad to provide the considerable funds a move like this required.

Keen to be close to his now elderly mother, Peace selected a smart property in the eastern suburb of Darnall, Sheffield. This was just a short walk from the home in Attercliffe to which his dear mother had relocated some years before. Another benefit of the move was that Peace was now within walking distance of a small, usually unmanned train platform, from which he could embark upon his regular journeys unnoticed,

Darnall was still a working class neighbourhood; Peace would have selected nothing else despite his new found wealth, but with a bigger new home came new bigger hopes and grander dreams. This was to be fresh start, with a new home, new furniture, and new neighbours.

Chapter 4

Romance and Retribution

'My heart is set, as firmly as ever heart of man was set on woman.
I have no thought, no view, no hope, in life beyond her; and if
you oppose me in this great stake, you take my peace and
happiness in your hands, and cast them to the wind.'
Charles Dickens , Author, 1812-1870

Arthur Dyson was an extremely tall man, even by today's standards. Yet, his 6'5" frame carried with it very little in the way of excess bulk, he was as thin as a rake, and carried himself with every ounce of the sober gentility expected of a Victorian middle class gentleman. His expensive suits were immaculately pressed, and his air of silent superiority marked him as aloof and unapproachable throughout his neighbourhood.

Much of his public persona was self-created, as Arthur Dyson was a working man, albeit an educated worker with a history of lower management positions. Since his arrival in Darnall, Sheffield, in early 1874, he had found himself to be a man between two worlds; too educated and important to mix with the manual labourers who resided in the area, yet too lowly to join the upper echelons of Sheffield's high society.

His airs and graces were born of a middle-class upbringing, which was by now largely redundant, as he lived and worked cheek by jowl with his working class neighbours. Yet there had been some considerable wealth in his family at one time, as Arthur Dyson had previously travelled to America where he had lived and worked for a number of years.

It was during his time in Cleveland, Ohio, that Dyson met the woman who was to be the love of his life. Katherine, known as Kate by those close to her, was a young Irish girl, who had also been relocated across the Atlantic with her middle-class parents. Described as "tall, buxom, and blooming", this was a modest young lady who refused to be judged solely on her obvious charms, preferring to rely on her natural wit and intellect to make her way in life.

Kate seemed to be the perfect partner for a serious and earnest young man like Arthur Dyson. She was beautiful without being overly obvious, and was clever and opinionated, without being deemed unruly and awkward, traits which were viewed as being unfavourable in a young woman by the Victorian middle-classes.

Dyson had worked with railway companies for the majority of his adulthood, and found plenty of work in the ever-growing United States, since the railways were constantly being extended upon the creation of every new settlement between the affluent and cultured east, and the wild and largely unoccupied open spaces of the west.

It was to be an offer of employment from a British railway company that eventually ended the love affair between Dyson and his adopted homeland. His success overseas had been a welcome factor in his extended stay, but given his desire for social acceptance he longed to rejoin British society, and raise a family amidst the genteel familiarity of his home nation.

However, there was a darker side to this match made in heaven. Behind her sweet Sunday school persona, Kate Dyson was more than a little fond of strong drink - a secret which may have played a part in their relocation to the UK. It is more than possible that Arthur Dyson had decided to move these marital problems away from the prying eyes of his prim and proper parents.

Those who knew the couple would later reveal that arguments were commonplace between Arthur and Kate, with Kate's drinking and Arthur's controlling manner usually being the main cause of these regular hostilities. Yet, the same folk would also add that there was a great deal of affection between the two, despite the frequent quarrelling.

By the time the couple had made the move across the Atlantic and settled in Sheffield, they were the proud parents of an infant son. The pleasures of parenthood had gone a long way to healing many of the rifts between the two and, as a family they began their new life with zeal and genuine hope that this was to be a new beginning for the ambitious and respectable Dyson family.

Unfortunately for the family, their rediscovered marital bliss was not to last. By 1875, the Dysons had settled into the suburb of Darnall, just a couple of miles east of the centre of Sheffield. Although they very rarely mixed with the other residents of Britannia Road, they had made a home to be proud of, and maintained an agreeable level of domestic bliss.

However, it would be this desire to create a smart and fashionable home that would introduce the couple to the man who would threaten their marriage and start a downward spiral of events which would eventually prove catastrophic for the young couple. All it took to light the touch paper was a rare and uncharacteristic attempt to be friendly with the neighbours. Unfortunately, the Dysons had no idea of the company they were about to keep.

The family who had recently moved into the house next-door-but-one to their own had appeared to be respectable enough, and it was with interest that Arthur Dyson came to learn that the man of the house was a picture framer by trade. House-proud as ever, the couple decided that some of their paintings could benefit from reframing, and with this, the decision was made to commission their close neighbour to do the work for them.

Calling at the house one evening, Arthur was pleasantly surprised to find himself in the company of a man with a great passion for the arts, and an obvious love of animals. During their polite conversation, it had been instantly agreed that the man would reframe the paintings at a favourable rate. Before long, Dyson headed home and wasted no time in singing the praises of the friendly and intelligent nature of their new neighbour, the affable Mr Charles Peace.

It was not long before Dyson and Peace came as close to being friends as Arthur Dyson was capable of. Many evenings were spent in the home of Charlie and Hannah, where the man of the house would entertain his guest by playing one of his many musical instruments, or engage his neighbour in deep discussion over current affairs, religion, and the arts.

The work for which Peace had been paid in advance was also completed quickly and to a very high standard, with which his paying customer was extremely impressed. Three paintings now hung in the Dyson home, resplendent in their glistening new frames, all the time reminding Arthur Dyson of the eccentric, yet fascinating man with whom he had become acquainted.

Peace and his wife were soon invited to the Dyson home for an evening of music and discussion, an invitation which the new couple in the area accepted with great pleasure. This had been the chance of a new start, a new respectable life, and never could the couple have dreamed of having close friends of such good character.

On one particular evening Peace was eventually formally introduced to Kate Dyson, an attractive young woman whom he had so far only glimpsed during the rare occasions on which she had left the house. The two appeared to get on famously from the outset, sharing interests in music, culture, and exotic animals.

From this evening onwards, Peace was a regular visitor to the household, often arriving unannounced to regale his friends with an amusing story, or a recital on a new instrument which had come into his possession. These early visits had brought joy into a home which had, until now, been bereft of music and laughter. This was particularly welcomed by the vivacious young Kate, who had spent the majority of her adulthood in the company of her sober and quiet husband.

However, things were beginning to move a little quickly for Arthur Dyson, a man who enjoyed the peace and quiet of his own company. The frequent visits and little gifts left for his wife were beginning to get out of hand. It had been nice to make a friend in the neighbourhood, but Dyson got the feeling that, like an over-affectionate dog, Peace would take some shaking off if he was to be left alone with his young family.

Initially, Dyson had sought to dissuade Peace from visiting as politely as possible, explaining that his young son was asleep, or that his wife was feeling unwell. However, this did little to calm the exuberance of their neighbour, and the visits continued until Dyson could take no more and directly asked Peace not to attend the house until further notice.

The straw that broke the camel's back was an unannounced visit in which Peace arrived during dinner, and failed to take his leave when strong hints were dropped that the family wished to dine in peace. It was on this very occasion that Arthur Dyson politely, yet firmly, asked his guest to refrain from visiting the family.

However, after their guest had submitted to Dyson's request, a row broke out between Arthur and Kate in regards to his cold treatment of their neighbour. Kate enjoyed the company of Mr Peace, and would not be forbidden from seeing him; this was wholly unacceptable to Dyson, who ordered his wife to refrain immediately from speaking to their neighbour, especially without his own presence.

Fortunately for Kate, her husband's work for the railway company meant that he would often be away until late at night, giving the bored young housewife the opportunity to spend time with their interesting and amusing neighbour. So Peace had got his way, and would continue to spend time in the presence of a lively young woman with time to listen to his anecdotes and impromptu recitals.

From this point onwards, Charlie and Kate would often be seen in each other's presence, often attending music hall concerts and local fairs together. The two made an odd couple; a small limping older man accompanied by a tall, pretty young woman. However, in the eyes of the world they were friends, and nobody would come between them, not even Arthur Dyson.

Kate had made a point of openly spending time with Peace, a fact which often enraged her husband. But, in a manner which was very rare at the time, Kate stood up to her husband, and refused to allow him to control her. If she were forbidden to see her friend, she would take their son and leave for America to rejoin her family.

It would appear then, that allowing his wife to spend time with their neighbour was the lesser of two evils for Dyson. He could risk a small amount of gossip owing to his wife being seen in the company of another man, or a huge scandal if Kate lived up to her threats and left him to return to Ohio. His only option was to acquiesce to his wife's demands.

As if the humiliation caused by seeing his young wife devote more and more time to her friendship with Peace wasn't enough, this neighbourly camaraderie also led to another problem in Arthur's life. Peace was renowned for being fond of drink, and as a result Kate Dyson, who had tried so hard recently to curb her alcohol intake, again fell foul of the temptations of the local pubs and drinking dens, most notably the Britannia pub, where she would often accompany Peace to his impromptu musical performances.

Arthur Dyson was at breaking point, and it was around this time that he was dealt a further blow. After failing to arrive at a railway station to which he had been assigned to perform his duties, Dyson was relieved of his post, and as a consequence was robbed of the small amount of social standing which the lower management job afforded him.

Later, many of Dyson's former colleagues and acquaintances would state that the cause of his erratic behaviour in the career to which he had previously been so devoted, was "domestic trouble", and that he had failed to attend his job on several occasions, each time having found his wife wandering around the neighbourhood in a drunken state.

However, despite the severe damage to her husband's reputation, Kate and Peace had become more inseparable than ever. The two were even photographed together at a local fair, much to the ire of Arthur Dyson. With his life spinning out of control, and with no easy means of regaining his reputation, it was time for Mr Dyson to put his foot down.

No longer employed, Dyson had begun to spend more and more time at the house, a fact which threatened to scupper the plans of his wife and their neighbour. At this point several notes were sent between Kate and Peace, notes which would one day be studied with interest, and their seemingly unimportant contents held under the spotlight for judgement.

With plenty of time on his hands since his unfortunate dismissal from work, Dyson began to devote his time to finding out exactly what kind of man Charlie Peace was; he had seemed too polite and friendly upon their earlier meetings, but since he was asked to refrain from visiting the house, something had changed; it seemed that this small act of defiance had released a demon into the streets of Darnall.

It did not take long for Dyson to receive word of Peace's frequent arrests and bouts of imprisonment. Not only was his wife consorting with someone he regarded as being "ungentlemanly", she was devoting her time to a criminal with a terrible reputation. As disconcerting as this news was to Arthur, this was, perhaps, the leverage he needed to finally wrench his wife from the grasp of Charlie Peace.

With no meaningful employment to lose, and an already battered reputation, Dyson could no longer stand by and watch this wretched man tear his family apart, and the only way in which he could be stopped was to convince the impressionable Kate of Peace's bad character. Should this not be enough to make her see reason, Arthur Dyson held another trick up his perfectly pressed sleeve.

ROMANCE AND RETRIBUTION

In consorting with a known criminal, Kate Dyson had left herself open to a number of problems, the most serious being that Arthur could now easily take away the child on which both parents doted. No court in the land would grant custody of a child to a mother with a drink problem and a reputation for associating with well-known nefarious characters.

Secondly, even if Kate were to live up to her threats and return to America, she would do so alone, and would be forced to explain to her family the reason for the break-up of her seemingly perfect marriage. She would be a woman disgraced by her own vices, and would more than likely be turned away from the genteel family home in which she was raised.

In a rare moment of triumph, Arthur Dyson, so frequently humiliated and downtrodden, now held all of the cards. There can be no doubt that he still loved his wife dearly, but desperate times called for drastic measures, and all he needed to do was to sit down with Kate during an increasingly rare moment of sobriety and allow the newly discovered facts to speak for themselves.

The forbidden friendship was also beginning to stir trouble in the Peace household, no doubt fuelled by the insistence of Charlie that his friend was to visit the family home on several occasions, much to the anger and humiliation of Hannah Peace. It has even been suggested that it was not uncommon for a drunken Kate Dyson to join the couple and their children at the dinner table.

Peace, for all of his repugnant qualities, was at least an intelligent man, and will no doubt have been awakened to his deplorable actions during a visit to his beloved mother. Jane Peace had always been a voice of reason to her son, and it was this close relationship that had often saved Charlie from his own actions.

Arriving at the home of his mother one afternoon, with a slurring and swaying Kate by his side, Peace had introduced his 'friend' to the elderly and astute Jane, who had immediately dismissed the drunken and overly familiar young woman, and given her frequently troublesome son a substantial piece of her mind.

Unperturbed by this motherly lecture, Peace was keen to maintain his friendship with the young, attractive married woman with whom he had shared so many raucous drinking sessions and trips to the music halls.

49

However, things were beginning to clear in the gin-soaked mind of Kate Dyson - perhaps this was her first outing on the road to ruin?

Having already been on the receiving end of Jane Peace's indignation, and no doubt having received similar outbursts from Hannah Peace, it would appear that, by June 1876, the friendship was beginning to cool, if only from Kate's perspective. Peace, as always, was adamant that nothing would be refused to him, even going as far as telling a friend of his *'if I make up my mind to a thing, I am bound to have it.'*

Having seen the error of her recent actions, Kate was becoming more and more sensible as every day without her disreputable consort passed. From later evidence, it would appear that the threats which were tucked away up the sleeve of her husband were never required, as on hearing of Peace's criminal past, she had vowed to put an end to the friendship which had almost led her to a life of ruin and disgrace.

Upon his next visit to the house, Kate had curtly informed Peace that she was no longer permitted to spend time with him, and that their relationship had been unwise and damaging to the reputations of all involved. Watching her close friend walk away, Kate could be forgiven for thinking that this was an end to a period of unrest; however, this was the beginning of a feud which would have dire consequences for the Dyson family.

For days following this humiliating experience, Peace continued to hammer on the door of the Dyson home, demanding to see Kate. This was a man who was not used to being deprived of anything and the situation of being discarded in such a blunt manner was almost too much for him to bear. His feelings of friendship, and possibly love, had now made way for furious anger and resentment.

By the end of the month, it would appear that the constant door-knocking and flurry of unanswered notes sent by Peace had driven Arthur Dyson to a state of uncharacteristic fury, and he knew that it was time to make his feelings on the matter clear to the unwonted visitor. He had allowed his wife to dissolve the friendship on her terms, but the time had come to add his influence to the current state of affairs.

In a manner which could only be seen as confrontational by a genteel Victorian gentleman, Arthur Dyson decided that the best way to be rid of this unwonted pest was to pen a note of his own, a note so passive and polite in its nature, that the brief contents would forever be remembered in the story of Charlie Peace. Written on a visiting card and dropped into the garden of his neighbour, the famous note read:

'Charles Peace is requested not to interfere with my family.'

As inconsequential, and possibly cowardly, as this note would seem today, this was a serious affront to the recipient of the card. This was a direct, not public, threat, which, to a man like Charles Peace, could not be ignored. Like the visiting card, *he* had been thrown aside with a blatant lack of dignity, and would go to any lengths available to even the score with his prim and proper neighbour.

From this day onwards, the relationship between the neighbours became a verbal battleground with Peace taking every opportunity to make caustic remarks and thinly-veiled threats whenever he met his foe in the street. For his part, Arthur Dyson responded with silent distaste at these exchanges, something which, to Peace, was more insulting than any threat.

The friction between the households continued in earnest, and in an interview which Kate would later give to the Sheffield Independent, the true extent of Peace's harassment of the Dysons was revealed.

'We couldn't get rid of him. I can hardly describe all that he did to annoy us after he was informed that he was not wanted at our house. He would come and stand outside the window at night and look in, leering all the while.

He had a way of creeping and crawling about, and of coming upon you suddenly unawares. He wanted me to leave my husband, but he was a demon, beyond even the power of a Shakespeare to paint.'

Matters were to take an ugly turn one Saturday in July, when, upon coming across his sworn enemy in the street, Peace casually, yet intentionally, tripped his neighbour in full view of several local residents. However, shaking with anger and burning with rage, Dyson managed to maintain his remaining dignity and walk away, refusing to dignify Peace's childish actions with retaliation.

Having seen first hand the 'demon' with which she had been involved, Kate was now firmly on the side of her husband against their tormentor. Upon being told of the incident of that afternoon, she had stepped out onto the street that evening to complain of Peace's behaviour to other neighbours, failing to notice the limping man who was now within earshot of her conversation.

Upon seeing the oncoming Peace, the neighbours quickly walked away, leaving Kate to face her livid neighbour alone. A quarrel ensued, an argument which would have dire consequences for Peace, and would see the previously trivial feud escalate into a much more serious chain of events.

Without warning, the furious Peace reached into his pocket and produced a revolver, which he held to the forehead of his former friend, who had become frozen with fear. 'I will blow your bloody brains out, and your husband's too!' screamed Peace, before concealing the weapon once again, and hurriedly fleeing through the door of his own house.

Kate Dyson was terrified and dashed into the safety of her home, into the arms of the husband who had been so grievously mistreated by herself and the man who had just threatened their lives on their very doorstep. Peace had been pushed too far, and had now, due to his inability to control his violent temper, given the upper hand to his enemies.

The police were immediately summoned, and listened with interest to Kate Dyson's version of events. Peace was well known to the police, and it was a matter of minutes before they were knocking on the door of his house, demanding that the occupier make himself known and step out into the street.

No response came from the house, and no signs of life could be seen through the windows. The police forced entry into the premises, only to be greeted by an empty house, its contents having been left in situ like the deserted *Marie Celeste*. Peace had gone, along with his wife and children.

A warrant was issued immediately for Peace's arrest yet, like the crew of the ghost ship, he had vanished into thin air leaving behind no clues as to his whereabouts. For now, the Dysons could live without fear of intimidation, free from their tormentor, for whom there would be immediate arrest should he approach the house again.

Days and weeks passed, with no sightings of the mischievous Peace being reported. However, around this time, it would appear that Mrs Hannah Peace had been busy, as she was now the owner of a run-down eating house in a working class area of Hull, where she lived with her children. The whereabouts of her husband was unknown.

The lease of the shop had been paid in cash by Mrs Peace, and after several visits by the police, she had convinced the constables that she no longer knew the whereabouts of her husband, who had left her to look after their offspring alone and would not be returning to Hull. Her husband had disgraced the family and was no longer welcome to take his place as head of the household.

Yet, hidden away in an upstairs room sat a man, brooding on his humiliation and plotting revenge against those who had seen him run out of his hometown by the police. He had lost a battle but would be ready for the war. All he had to do was bide his time and keep out of sight.

And as for the tormented Dyson family? They had finally been freed of the demon that plagued their lives, but had decided to take further precautions in guarding themselves against interference and harassment. In a matter of weeks, the family had packed up their belongings, said goodbye to Darnall, and found themselves a new home on the other side of the city.

Chapter 5

Three Irish Brothers

'Justice is itself the great standing policy of civil society; and any eminent departure from it, under any circumstances, lies under the suspicion of being no policy at all.'
Edmund Burke, Irish Statesman, 1729-1797

A mysterious journey, from the East Riding of Yorkshire to the outskirts of the industrial city of Manchester, had brought Charlie Peace to the leafy, outlying area of Whalley Range. Now a thriving suburb of the north-west's most populous city, but in 1876 the area was largely made up of a few modest rows of houses which merely interrupted the panorama of the Lancashire countryside. This wasn't the kind of place where outsiders were welcomed, yet the village had seen a few new arrivals in recent days and weeks.

The long-suffering Hannah Peace had been left to run the family's latest business venture, spending her days preparing food and cooking in the eating house which her husband had seen fit to buy on their sudden arrival in Hull. The real reason for her husband's cross-Pennine venture has never been proven, but he had vaguely informed his wife that he was travelling to Manchester 'on business', giving no indication of when he would return, or any details regarding the true purpose of this impromptu business trip.

Given the prolific criminal career of Charlie Peace, it does not require too much of a stretch of the imagination to assume that the remote, yet modestly wealthy homes of the local farmers and shopkeepers were the 'business' to which Peace had to attend. Being a good few miles from the city, and with the whole of the surrounding countryside to escape into should any of his frequent nocturnal misdemeanours be discovered, it would seem that Peace had found himself the perfect location in which to line his pockets, and the coffers of his new, legitimate business in Hull.

THREE IRISH BROTHERS

As was routine for Peace, his arrival in town had turned no heads. This outwardly flamboyant and unique character had long since recognised the importance of anonymity, and as such deliberately sought to slip into Whalley Range relatively unnoticed. For now, sobriety and understatement were the order of the day. This was just a suited and bespectacled businessman, quietly going about his work. Whenever Peace travelled 'on business', he was the man that nobody noticed.

Unwittingly aiding Peace in his attempts at anonymity, another group of visitors to Whalley Range had arrived in the area some months before, and despite their legitimate employment as farm labourers, they were certainly not unknown to the residents, especially the inn-keepers and policemen, who knew each of the three men by name. By all accounts, when the sun set over the farms and work was finished for the day, it was time to batten down the hatches and lock up the innocent and genteel daughters of the parish.

The three young men were brothers, Frank, John, and William Habron. They had travelled from their native Ireland in search of work and adventure. The work had been easy to come by, seasonal farm labourers were much in demand in the more rural outreaches of British towns, and these three strong young men certainly knew how to do an honest day's work. However, the adventure that would come their way would be of earth-shattering proportions, and result in the family name being recorded in the history books for eternity.

Their employer, a farmer by the name of Mr Deakin, had thought highly of the three brothers since their arrival on his farm, and even allowed them to lodge in a barn on his land during their stay. They were diligent and tireless workers, and he trusted these men enough to largely leave the running of his livelihood to them. However, in a small, tightly-knit community such as Whalley Range, stories travelled quickly, and it had been frequently noted that the night time brought out the demons in Frank, John and William.

Their destination of choice after a hard day's labour was the Royal Oak pub. Although the inn was usually the kind of quiet, homely establishment which one would expect to find in the rural areas of the north of England, when the Habrons paid a visit it was often reported to be more akin to a rowdy Wild West saloon. On several occasions, the police attended the premises only to find broken glass, blackened eyes and raucous singing.

Of the three, the youngest brother William was usually the ringleader of their nocturnal mayhem. Although John and Frank enjoyed their evenings of drink and debauchery just as much, it was William who was always the first to raise his fists. Being a tall, powerfully built young man, there were usually no takers when William offered a fight to anyone unfortunate enough to have been in his path, but on one particular night he found himself a willing sparring partner amongst the men of Whalley Range.

It was a Saturday night, 31st July, 1876, and the bar was busy with weekend drinkers. On nights like this, the Habrons were less likely to be kept an eye on by the inn-keeper, although it was a regular occurrence for the local policemen to look into the establishment on their rounds when the brothers were in attendance.

The reputation of the brothers, added to the apparent need for a regular patrol of the premises, would lead many to believe that the proprietor of the pub was keen to keep a tight rein on his rowdier customers, but also relied on their regular custom. Barring three men who seemed to be more than happy to pass their week's wages over the bar would have been a bad decision for any business.

Constable Nicholas Cock was well known to the publican of the Royal Oak, and to his customers. He poked his head around the door for the first time that night at around 10pm, and was surprised to see no signs of trouble amongst the drunken clientele. The pub was rowdy and busy, but the atmosphere seemed to be one of good-natured revelry. However, on seeing William Habron in a state of drunkenness, Constable Cock decided to make another visit as his round brought him back to the pub.

A week earlier he had been called to the premises by the landlord, and had arrived to find William letting fly with his powerful fists after an argument with a local man. The fight itself was quickly stopped, and the quarrel calmed; however, it would appear that William was not a man who enjoyed being publically admonished.

This was by no means the first time the somewhat zealous and youthful Nicholas Cock had been forced to intervene in the Habrons' unruly behaviour, and he knew it was time to put his foot down with the ringleader of the Royal Oak revellers.

Having dispersed the excitable crowd and separated the two protagonists, Constable Cock turned to William, and jabbed an authoritative finger in his direction before threatening further punishment.

'Look here Habron, I'm tired of this. The next time you raise disorder here, I'll have you in front of the Magistrate.'

The fact that fighting seems to have been a regular occurrence, yet this was the first threat to William Habron of ending up in the dock, seems to suggest that the behaviour of the young Irishman had been tolerated thus far, and seen as a petty annoyance to the inhabitants of the community. However, a line always has to be drawn but this was not recognised, and was taken as a challenge to the bravado of young William.

He was being challenged by a man only four years his senior in front of an audience and in his state of drunkenness, combined with his need to retain dignity in front of his opponent and his brothers, this threat could not be taken without rebuttal. Here he was, towering above the averagely-built bobby who had so publically chastised him. He had no choice but to reply with a threat of his own - a threat that would come back to haunt him in a very short space of time.

'It'll be a sorry day for you, the day you arrest me.'

Returning to the pub a week later for the second time, Constable Cock will no doubt have been reminded of his threat towards William Habron a week earlier, and would also have remembered the warning he received in response, especially as on his approach to the inn, the night air was filled with the tell-tale sounds of shouting, swearing, and glass being broken. If Habron was involved, Cock had no choice but to act on his previous warning, and knew that even subduing this habitual miscreant was difficult in itself, let alone detaining him until he could be seen by the magistrate.

Constable Cock would have prayed it wasn't Habron who was the cause of the commotion, for this time matters would have to be taken further, and that would also involve the intervention of John and Frank. There was no way on earth the two other Habron boys would allow their brother to be taken by the police. It would be wise to wait for his colleague, Constable Beanland, to arrive before wading into the chaos wielding his truncheon.

Eventually, the two policemen entered the building to be greeted with a sight that surprised neither of them. William Habron and a burly local labourer were in the midst of a fistfight which was of such magnitude that the landlord of the pub feared for his furniture. With assistance from Constable Beanland and the fearful landlord, Cock eventually managed to place himself between the two men, while other locals held the protagonists back from one another.

Between them, Beanland and Cock managed to drag Habron back to their little station, situated just a stone's throw from the inn, and placed him in the cells until he could be brought before the magistrate. However, on this rare occasion, many witnesses to the brawl insisted that, unusually, Habron had been the injured party. Almost the entire crowd of onlookers had spared Habron of any blame, instead reporting that the burly labourer had picked on Habron in his unusually sober state, eager to be known as the man who beat the Irishman at his own confrontational game.

It would appear that Habron may have taken some notice of Cock's threat the previous week, and his brothers, along with other drinkers from the Royal Oak, had insisted that William had behaved impeccably for the entire evening, even slowing down his usually rapid and voluminous intake of alcohol. But, Cock had made a promise, and he had decided to let the magistrate be the judge of whether Habron should shoulder the blame for one too many nights of violence and debauchery.

This was to prove a very unfortunate decision, as the very next day (which was a Sunday, so would suggest that the matter was dealt with as a matter of urgency), the magistrate in nearby Chorlton-cum-Hardy ordered that Habron be released immediately after listening intently to the testimony of the many hung-over witnesses.

Feeling not only slighted by being arrested by his nemesis, but also angry that, for once, he was not to blame for the incident in which he had been implicated, Habron strode from the dock and pushed the group of spectators aside, before standing eye to eye with Constable Cock, and delivering another chilling warning for all to hear.

'I promised you a sorry day if you ever ran foul of me. I'll do you in for this!'

This was a threat that many would remember, being so publically delivered in front of the magistrate himself. It would appear that the only soul in the courtroom to be dismissive of such a warning was Cock himself, who retorted to his opponent with a sense of dismissal and boredom.

'Oh, you're all bluster and wind...I know you.'

And with that, the ever-diligent Constable Cock took his leave to return to his rounds. Little did anyone know that he would have only hours to live.

At ten to midnight, as his rounds were drawing to a close, Cock walked the streets of Whalley Range again with his colleague, James Beanland, and a law student named John Massey Simpson. The three paused for a while under the gaslight on a street corner, and chatted amiably about the events of the day, and no doubt the previous night, before Massey bid the two policemen goodnight, and began his short walk home.

It was at this point that Beanland was alerted by a noise in the distance, and saw what appeared to be a stooping man, furtively entering the unoccupied property of a local businessman, Mr John Gratrix. Keen not to alert the man to their presence until they were close enough to apprehend him, the two men split up and quietly approached the area in which they had seen the mysterious man enter the grounds of the house. The two drew ever nearer, circling their suspect, trapping him at the scene of a crime.

Unfortunately for Cock, it was he who had reached the suspect first, and found a man trying to conceal himself in the darkness. Their eyes met for a brief moment, before the intruder took to his heels and tried to flee the scene. The youthful Nicholas Cock was too quick for the stooping man and blocked his escape, only to find himself staring down the barrel of a hastily produced revolver.

As dedicated to his job as ever, Cock propelled himself towards the armed intruder only to be shot at. This first shot had been a warning, and had sailed deliberately wide of the young policeman. Failing to take heed and allow the man to pass, Cock made a decision that was to cost him his life. He would stop at nothing to apprehend the man who had fired at him in the darkness. A second shot rang out and this was not a warning. The bullet had entered Cock's chest and knocked him off his feet. He collapsed into the mud instantaneously.

Wasting no time, the assailant fled like a scalded cat, vanishing into the darkness of the Lancashire countryside. With his final breaths and remaining strength, twenty-three year old Nicholas Cock yelled into the night:

'Murder...I'm shot...I'm shot.'

The two gunshots had caused John Massey to turn on his heels and race towards the commotion, and as he approached, he heard a shrill whistle for assistance, blown desperately into the air by Constable Beanland. He arrived to find the life rapidly draining from his friend, and Beanland helplessly attempting to stop the flow of blood from his colleague's wounds.

Just a short time later, the body of Constable Cock became calm and still. He was removed by a horse and cart to the premises of a local doctor, Dr Dill, but died before his superior officer could arrive. He had been tragically killed in the line of duty and somebody would be made to pay for this heinous act of murder.

The two men were soon joined by Police Superintendent Bent, who had been alerted by the whistle of Constable Beanland. Wasting no time in trying to apprehend his constable's killer, Bent asked Beanland to describe the man whom they had followed into the grounds of the house. Being sure only of a brown coat and a commonly worn pot hat, Beanland made a statement which, whether out of revenge or an innocent mistake given the darkness and confusion of the events, would pervert the course of justice for both the attacker, and the case as a whole.

'I suspect it is Will Habron.'

Unfortunately for all involved, the only man present who had seen the man in close proximity was now dead, his lifeless head cradled in the firelight of the doctor's parlour by the colleague who would stop at nothing to see justice brought to the killer of his friend. If Cock had been able to speak, he would have confirmed that the man who fired at him so cruelly was a good deal older than William Habron, and nowhere near as powerfully built. In fact, he was a man so rich in unusual features that he would have been apprehended almost immediately if anyone had been able to describe him.

The dark night was quickly lit by lamplight and burning torches as a small army of policemen and local residents strode through Whalley Range towards the farmland of the unassuming Mr Deakin. This was a witch-hunt, and the mob wanted blood for the murder of such a dedicated and diligent young police officer. Somebody was going to hang for this, whether by the laws of the land, or at the hands of the shocked and outraged townsfolk.

Upon reaching the outhouse which was home to the Habron brothers, an opinion was formed that a member of such a close knit family would not have acted alone in exacting retribution towards a man who had damaged their family pride. All three brothers would be arrested, and the guilty party would be discovered after it was ascertained who was a killer and who was an accomplice.

In an unfortunate indication of guilt, a candle which burned inside the barn was quickly extinguished as the hastily assembled army of witch-finders approached the building. The gang fanned out and surrounded the last bastion of protection afforded to the three labourers, as Superintendent Bent sent Mr Deakin into the barn to nervously check that his employees were in situ, before sweeping in behind him and bellowing towards the trio of marked men:

'William Habron, John Habron, Frank Habron, I arrest you in the name of the law for the murder of Constable Cock! We are armed and will shoot unless you light up and show you mean to give no trouble.'

With hands raised in the air, the colour drained from their normally ruddy faces, the three men slowly and cautiously arose from their beds. Protesting weakly that they had been asleep the whole time, they knew that they had no chance of escape and that their hopes lay in the hands of

Justice herself. Their only option was to co-operate, and tell their story to those who would decide their fate. The three were immediately transported to the nearby Old Trafford Police Station, Manchester, where they would be held until trial.

In a rare attempt at forensic analysis during the Victorian era, the decision was made to gather up the clothes and boots of the suspects. These would be examined thoroughly and presented at the trial should the need arise. Enquiries were also made, and when asked to describe a man who had asked for the price of some revolver cartridges on the day of the murder, two local clerks had stated that the man *could* have been the unfortunate William Habron.

While the brothers languished in gaol, Superintendent Bent had made something of a discovery. Returning to the scene of the murder with one of William Habron's boots, he discovered that a footprint close to the spot where Constable Cock had been discovered closely resembled the tread of the boot which he had brought for just such a purpose. However, the manufacturing of the boots had been fairly common, and no impressions or imprints were taken. Despite the tenuous nature of this discovery, the boot was tagged and included within an ever-growing arsenal of evidence against William Habron.

Another cruel twist of fate was to befall the unfortunate suspect, as percussion caps from a gun were found in the pocket of a waistcoat which had been worn by William that very night. The chains of justice were beginning to tighten around this frightened, nineteen year old Irishman, and by the time the trial arrived, he was named as the prime suspect amongst the three.

The courtroom was packed for this case as such a needless and cruel murder of a dedicated police officer had filled the local area with rage and revulsion. Reporters from all over the country descended on Manchester, along with witnesses and the intrigued public, one of whom was a stooping gentleman with a pronounced limp and wild, staring eyes. He attended every day of the trial, and listened intently as the damning array of evidence was presented.

In the face of such a strong prosecution case, the defence made a valiant attempt to refute the charges brought against the brothers, and Frank Habron was released without charge, since there was no evidence whatsoever to link him to the murder. He was released into society without a job, a home, or his two dear brothers.

William and John stood side by side in the dock, and being poorly educated and barely literate, the prosecution found cross-examination to be easy. In a short space of time, the two terrified men had contradicted their story of events, and the prosecution barristers were ready to pounce upon every forced mistake and every slight variation in the statements of the two prisoners.

It would seem that the only ally the two remaining Habrons had was their former employer, Mr Deakin, who had always been full of praise for his labourers, even defending their behaviour during those wild and debauched nights in Whalley Range. He emphatically informed those present that the two, especially William, were hard-working and honest employees, and even testified that the waistcoat in which the percussion caps were found had belonged to him, and had been loaned to William on that fateful day.

The damning boot was then produced and although the judge, Mr Justice Lindley, and his jury had seen no imprint or photograph of this vital evidence, they appear to have been more than happy to take Superintendent Bent's word for it that the boot matched the muddy footprint at the scene of the crime. They asked no questions in regards to the validity of a piece of evidence which could only be compared to a long washed away footprint.

The main piece of evidence was the final nail in the coffin of William Habron. The public threat he had made to Constable Cock in a much smaller courtroom just a few miles away had come back to haunt him, and this was something which the defence counsel could not counter. Their only argument was that this was an unfortunate coincidence. This was summarily dismissed by the judge, who refused to believe that such a coincidence could occur, especially as the threat was made on the morning of the murder in question. And on this note, the trial was halted for deliberation.

After a few days of weighing up the overwhelming circumstantial evidence, the proceedings were reopened in Manchester and the crowds once again flocked to the courtroom. The first business of the day was for the judge to turn to the jury and ask them to decide the future of John

Habron. The jury had voted unanimously that John be released, so he was found not guilty and allowed to join his brother Frank in returning to lawful society.

Not so fortunate was William. The powerful array of evidence against him had been too strong for the defence counsel to credibly argue against. He was found guilty, but being of tender years, a recommendation of mercy was made in a token attempt to save his young life. 'I am innocent' was the desperate reply of William Habron, but his plea had once again fallen upon deaf ears. The judge donned his black cap and sentenced the terrified young man to death.

Nobody present in the courtroom was shocked; this was exactly the outcome the gathered observers had expected and hoped for. There was to be no surprise reprieve. Indeed the day had progressed with very little in the way of drama. Only a small scuffle at the beginning of the proceedings had raised any eyebrows, and this was at an agitated attempt to secure a front row seat by a strange looking man appearing older than his years and with a pronounced limp, who raised his voice in the hushed courtroom:

'Out of my way! I came all the way from Sheffield to see this trial!'

Chapter 6

Bullets Fly in Banner Cross

'He that studieth revenge keepeth his own wounds green,
which otherwise would heal and do well.'
John Milton, Poet, 1608-1674

tepping down from the train carriage on 29 November and losing himself in the bustling railway station crowd, Peace was no doubt buoyed by his remarkable, yet callous escape from the law in Manchester. He had been the recipient of a huge slice of good fortune during his time across the Pennines and no doubt sought to try his luck even further in the familiar streets of Sheffield.

The main Sheffield train station was itself the very same building which now stands just east of the city centre, having been opened in 1870 by the Midland Railway. In a telling sign of the times, the station had separate entrances and exits for each class of passenger, and it is fascinating to ponder from which exit Charlie Peace emerged into the bosom of his hometown.

One would expect that a man fleeing the murder of a policeman would choose the anonymity of third class travel, but with Peace's talent for disguise and brazen boldness, along with a pocket which was always lined by his ill-gotten gains; it is not beyond the realms of reality to imagine this small, wiry man consciously concealing his trademark limp and calmly strolling through the first class exit with the air of a respectable businessman.

Ever the dutiful son, Peace's first stop was at the home of his mother, Jane, who was surprised to receive this unexpected visit from her beloved, yet troublesome, youngest son. When asked why he had returned to Sheffield (his mother had believed him to still be in Hull with his wife and family) he told her that he had returned to attend a fair which was taking place that evening. However, it is clearly revealed by his later movements why Peace had returned, and after this flying visit to his long-suffering mother, he walked through the city centre, this time heading in a different direction.

Peace seems to have wasted no time in covering the two mile journey from the city centre to the western Sheffield district of Banner Cross, arriving there in the early afternoon. His journey would have taken him along what is now the busy and cosmopolitan Ecclesall Road, lined with artisan cafes and independent shops.

However, in 1876, this area was mostly residential and home to an eclectic mix of working class terraced houses, and the villas of the wealthy and entitled. He would have known this area like the back of his gnarled and deformed hand, due to the large number of prosperous homes in the area, many of which he would have entered unlawfully during his frequent burglary sprees.

By the time one reaches Banner Cross from this direction, the city architecture seems to have thinned somewhat, and glimpses of the surrounding countryside can be seen between the more generously spaced buildings. The architecture of Ecclesall Road and Banner Cross have changed very little in the years since Peace limped his way towards his illicit and forbidden companion, Kate Dyson and the quieter streets of Banner Cross would have been a welcome sight to a man intent on having his revenge on the family which had pushed him away. He was the bad penny who would keep turning up on their respectable doorstep and his recent good fortune had seemingly rendered him more brazen than ever before.

It had actually not been long since Peace had visited this part of Sheffield. He had made flying visit just a few weeks previously, again from 'business' in Manchester, just in time to welcome his former neighbours to their new home. As the unsuspecting family arrived in the street with their belongings packed into horse drawn carts, they had been astonished and disgusted to see the grinning face of Charlie Peace as he stood on their doorstep with the intention of causing nuisance.

'You see, I am here to annoy you, wherever you go' had been his mischievous greeting, and only when a threat was made to bring a policeman did Peace again leave the area, to attend the culmination of an important trial in Manchester.

BULLETS FLY IN BANNER CROSS

Upon reaching the Dyson's neighbourhood again, Peace must have decided to give Kate one more chance to rekindle their illicit affair. He penned a note in which he asked his former lover to meet him in secret and asked a local woman, Mrs Sarah Colgrave, to deliver the note to the Dyson house.

No doubt fearful and dubious of the intentions of this strange looking little man and his unusual request, Mrs Colgrave flatly refused to assist in his amorous endeavours and took her leave of this opportunistic lothario, threatening to bring the police if he persisted in pestering her. Her account of this unusual encounter would later be recounted in a nearby pub, but certainly not in the form of idle chatter over a pint of ale.

Coincidentally, another local pub, the Banner Cross Hotel (a large Tudor fronted public house which still stands proudly at the far end of Ecclesall Road) was to be Peace's next port of call. No doubt thirsty after a day of travelling, he approached the building with drink, merriment and mischief on his mind.

Ever the showman, he spent the afternoon and early evening in good spirits, even performing an ad hoc show for the congregated afternoon drinkers with the aid of a sturdy stick, a piece of wire and an iron poker fashioned into a crude percussion instrument. He skilfully tapped at the dangling poker with the stick, beating out melodies to the delight of his fellow patrons.

Until this point, the day seems to have been somewhat relaxed and jolly. But things were to change as Peace eventually left the comfort of the pub. Whether he had outstayed his welcome, run out of money, or made a conscious decision to leave the warmth of the pub to take care of other business on this chilly November evening is unknown, but the details of a strange conversation which was to take place under a gas lantern outside the premises, were certainly well documented in the coming days and weeks.

Charles Brassington, a local labourer, was standing in the gaslight as he was approached by an unusual stranger who appeared from the gloom and joined him beneath the lantern. The strange man immediately began a conversation which quickly steered deliberately towards the Dyson family.

Brassington attempted to avoid conversation as he was wary of the strange looking man, stating that he didn't know the family as they were still new to the area. However, the stranger persisted, making several derogatory claims as to the financial problems and moral standing of the seemingly respectable family.

When Brassington showed no interest in the subject at hand, Peace went on to produce from his pocket a collection of notes and letters which he claimed were proof of the Dysons' secret marital difficulties and financial irregularities.

The contents of these letters, however, were hopelessly lost on the annoyed and disinterested Charles Brassington, as he took one glance at them and informed the man that he couldn't read, which was certainly not uncommon at the time (although, illiterate or not, there was certainly nothing wrong with this witness's vision or memory, as he was later, with the aid of a recent photograph, to identify the mysterious stranger who approached him under the gaslight as the infamous Charlie Peace).

No doubt annoyed by the reluctance of the wary labourer to listen to his bitter allegations, Peace then called on the vicar of Ecclesall, Reverend Newman. Peace had actually visited the vicar around five weeks previously, shortly before he had embarked on his eventful trip across the Pennines to Manchester. During their first meeting, Reverend Newman had listened patiently to Peace's allegations against the family, and his claims that he had been driven from his home by his mistreatment at the hands of the Dysons.

Reverend Newman had listened calmly as was his profession, and had asked Peace to provide proof of this alleged mistreatment. It was on this basis that Peace had now returned to the vicarage, with pockets stuffed with letters, calling cards and photographs, many of which contained the educated handwriting of Kate Dyson.

Later testimony from Reverend Newman reveals a sense of forgiveness by Peace towards Kate, but his anger and malicious intent towards Arthur were plain to see. He vowed to seek retribution and admitted to the vicar that he fully intended to take action against his perceived mistreatment. He even admitted that he would be immediately attending the Dyson home in order to 'take proceedings further.'

Eventually, the clergyman was able to calm his volatile visitor and Peace assured the vicar that he would not visit the family on that particular evening, but would instead visit his friend, John Gregory, who lived next door to the family in Banner Cross Terrace. No doubt Reverend Newman knew this to be an unwise choice, but was more than likely glad to see the back of his irate visitor by this point.

In a cruel twist of fate for Arthur Dyson, Mr Gregory was not at home. This led to Charlie Peace, filled with drink and rage, angrily pacing the pavement of Banner Cross Terrace. The temptation of paying a visit to the Dyson home was far too great. Here he was, just a few feet from the house of his sworn enemy and his ex-companion. However, this time, Peace would not stand grinning from ear to ear on the doorstep for the entire neighbourhood to see.

He bided his time and watched the rear of the house from a dark passage which led to the backs of each terraced house on the row. With his long history of burglaries, Peace was no stranger to waiting in the cold and dark for a moment of opportunity, he had watched hundreds of houses waiting for the moment that the coast was clear and this occasion was no different.

By this time, Kate was joining her husband in the parlour having put their young son to bed. By all accounts, the couple had by now settled their differences and were more united than ever in the face of the harassment aimed at the couple by the persistent Peace.

The houses of Banner Cross Terrace were relatively small, yet quite cosy and modern for the late nineteenth century, and the parlour would have been warm and inviting with an open fire. The only drawback was that these houses, like the vast majority during this time, had no inside toilet facilities, and in leaving the warmth of the parlour fire, and the companionship of her husband, Kate's life was to change forever as she made for the back door in order to use the outside privy.

A pair of beady eyes in the darkness watched her as she crossed the yard and entered the outbuilding, to be followed by a series of soft footsteps, vastly experienced in covering ground quickly and quietly in order not to raise any concerns or alarm, or give away any inkling of an oncoming threat. Peace was an expert at appearing in the most unexpected places and was already loitering with intent at the wooden privy door before Kate had finished her ablutions, ready and waiting to give her the fright of her life.

Without knowing she was about to be the victim of a terrifying approach and no doubt thinking about returning to the warm fire and the arms of her husband, Kate unlocked the door and stepped out into the chilly darkness. To her surprise and terror, upon leaving the outhouse, her eyes met the gaze of Charlie Peace, leering maniacally at her through the darkness.

This sight terrified Kate to her very core, and for a moment, the two stared at each other. Kate was rooted to the spot with terror and one could imagine that Peace was simply enjoying the fear in his former companion's expression. It was Peace who eventually broke the silence, his shouts piercing the silence of the quiet winter evening.

'Speak, or I'll fire!' he bellowed at the terrified woman who had been so effectively stalked on her own property. The tranquillity of the evening was again shattered, as Kate screamed with unbridled terror, staring at the revolver which was raised just inches from her colourless face. Taking the only action of self preservation available to her, Kate backed into the outhouse and locked the door, hoping that somebody had heard her cries and would come to her assistance.

The words 'Speak, or I'll fire!' are a telling indication of Peace's intentions in following Kate to the outhouse. Although he later claimed that his intention was to frighten the woman, the fact that he demanded that she speak to him itself speaks volumes as to the emotional turbulence which had led him to return to the house.

It is highly unusual for anyone who has stalked a victim to shout at them and alert other people in the vicinity. It is also unclear as to why Peace wanted so desperately for Kate to speak. Did he want an apology? Did he want her to explain herself?

It is not unlikely that Peace was hoping for a terrified Kate Dyson to admit her love for him, therefore proving to the world that he had been the victim of Kate's passion and Arthur's jealousy. There is no doubt that Peace certainly did regard himself as the victim in this series of events, and he was certain that Kate had been forced against her will to stay away from him. Perhaps if he could corner her with no chance of escape, he could learn the truth as to why he was so publicly cast aside by the Dyson family?

The reasons for Peace's choice of words will always remain a mystery, but there is a suggestion that the actual threat was misquoted during the ensuing investigation, and the threat was actually 'Speak, and I'll fire!' Although this small matter of a single word seems to be a little trivial in the grand scheme of things, it is this very word that changes the context of the threat, and with it, Peace's motive for approaching Kate in such a terrifying manner.

Despite the chilling and violent threat, Kate's screaming continued as she held onto the small amount of safety provided by the wooden outhouse door and its simple iron bolt. She did not speak to Peace, she did not say a single word, she simply screamed for her life in the confines of the dark privy.

Luckily for Kate, the outhouses of Banner Cross Terrace were not too far away from the terraced houses themselves and her startled husband, on hearing the terrified screams, had already bolted from his chair and was rushing through the yard towards the cries of his wife. On hearing Arthur's calls, she summoned every ounce of courage and dashed out of the privy through the darkness and towards her husband's rapidly approaching footsteps.

Whether his bravery had deserted him, or he had simply achieved the aims of his visit to the house, Peace turned on his heels and began to run away along the alleyway which the houses shared across the back of the terrace. Peace was a quick thinker and an athletic man, but due to the limp which had been with him since his days at the steel mill, he was certainly no sprinter. He knew he needed a head start on Kate's apoplectic husband who was by now just a few feet away from him.

Upon seeing the cause of his wife's screams, the anger felt by Arthur was apparent as he pushed past his trembling wife without a word and gave chase to the small, hobbling stalker who was rapidly disappearing down the alleyway. Dyson knew that he must put an end to this harassment, and would stop at nothing to apprehend their tormentor. All thoughts and concern as to his personal safety had seemingly been pushed aside by the rage and determination that led him to give chase through the darkness in pursuit of an armed and extremely dangerous man.

Following closely on the heels of his wife's attacker, Dyson sprinted through the alleyway from which Peace had trapped his prey just minutes before, just a few yards behind the man who had slipped into the night like a mischievous, malevolent sprite. As the two men bounded down a short flight of steps and into the street, one getting ever closer to the other, Peace had a quick decision to make, and the instinctive choice he made would alter one life forever and extinguish another.

Perfectly aware that he had no hope of out-running his pursuer, Peace had to take action while he remained ahead. He still had enough of a lead to turn and face his oncoming foe and in a stand-off, a man with a revolver always has the upper hand.

He stopped, turned and raised the gun, taking aim at the entrance to the alleyway, waiting for his target to emerge from the darkness. As Dyson's feet hit the cobbles at the bottom of the steps, Peace instantly fired towards his sworn enemy. The shot hit the wooden frame of the entrance, narrowly missing the rapidly approaching Arthur Dyson.

At this point, it would have been a normal reaction for Dyson to turn on his heels and disappear back up the steps towards the safety of his house. But, so consumed with rage must this much-tormented victim have been, that he continued to barrel towards Peace, his focus on nothing other than getting his hands on the man who threatened to tear his family apart, thus putting an end to the events which had threatened the privacy of his home and the stability of his marriage. If that meant putting himself in mortal danger, it seems that this was worth every risk for Arthur Dyson in those last few moments of madness.

Another shot rang out and this time Dyson's progress was permanently halted. His last chance to protect himself had passed; there was to be no escape from the second bullet. He dropped to the ground almost at the feet of his assassin and lay as still as a carved statue, a gaping scarlet hole in his forehead. The fateful second shot had entered his temple, and the brief, yet furious, chase was over.

The shots had disturbed the whole street and curtains opened as cries were heard from the inhabitants of the nearby houses. Raised voices surrounded the tragic scene, to be replaced almost instantly by cries of panic and confusion. Not for the first time in his life, Peace recognised that he must protect his precious freedom and hurriedly scampered into the night like a wily urban fox. He had quietly slipped away from another fatal shooting brought about by his very own trigger finger.

A trembling and terrified Kate Dyson had also run down the alleyway after the two men, no doubt desperate to keep her husband in sight and had reached the foot of the steps at the very moment the second shot rang out and her husband slumped to the ground.

Already hysterical and haunted by the events of the last few minutes, she found this final, terrible act of hatred towards herself and her dutiful husband too much to bear. She fell to her knees beside the prostrate body of Arthur and screamed hysterically at her evasive tormentor, bellowing into the cold November night:

'Murder! ...You villain! You have shot my husband!'

Chapter 7

'A Man of Very Bad Character'

'It is better to be the widow of a hero, than the wife of a coward.'
Dolores Ibarurri, Spanish Politician, 1895-1989

Arthur Dyson was dead. He had clung onto life long enough to be carried into the Banner Cross Hotel before being taken to his home. He died in the presence of his wife and a local surgeon in the parlour of his new home, the home which was intended to become a haven from the torment and interference of his eventual killer.

This was a case of unlawful killing, and as such, the police were brought to the scene immediately. However, their suspect had slipped into the darkness and escaped their clutches. A manhunt was called, and every police officer was charged with the duty of finding the killer of Arthur Dyson, and bringing him to justice. In the meantime, the official investigation into the murder was hastily begun.

In the Victorian era, the public inquest into an unlawful death was a critical part of the investigation. Just as in an actual trial, witnesses were called to give evidence, and any suspect was entitled, and usually forced, to be present. Unfortunately, this was an inquest which was to take place without a defendant.

Many believe the inquest into the death of Arthur Dyson took place at the Banner Cross Hotel, just yards from the spot where Peace fired the fatal shot. However, research into the inquest notes reveals this to be incorrect. The majority of these sombre proceedings were actually held at the Stag Inn, Sharrow Head, just a ten minute walk from the scene of the crime.

This official investigation was chaired by Mr Wightman, who was the Chief Coroner in Sheffield, and was attended by many members of the local community. Inquests were often held in public houses at this time, with the emphasis being that they were public inquests, and as such, The

74

Stag was commandeered as the venue in which one of Sheffield's most shocking events would be officially recounted.

The first day of the inquest (which did take place at the Banner Cross Hotel) on 1 December 1876, was a non-event. As Peace had slipped away into the night, and had not been seen or heard of since, the proceedings were postponed owing to the lack of a defendant. It would appear that, at this stage, the police were still confident in delivering their suspect into the clutches of justice.

Mr Wightman hushed those assembled, and addressed the attendees with an unusually heartfelt speech for an official occasion such as this. Inquests are usually conducted with a deliberate avoidance of human emotion, but it appears that the gravity of the events in Banner Cross had shocked not only the local community, but the whole of Sheffield.

'I need not explain to you why you are met here. This is a most lamentable case altogether. It appears that the man on whom suspicion rests, a man named Peace, whom in all probability you have all heard of, a man who is suspected in any rate of having caused the death of Arthur Dyson, is not in custody, and the whole affair is so recent that I am exceedingly sorry to say that I must adjourn the inquest.

I know it is exceedingly grievous to the relations of the deceased, and if I could have seen some way to fulfil my duty and at the same time complete the inquiry, I should have been very glad to have done so. But it is clear, it does not admit of a moment's doubt, that the matter is not thoroughly ripe for consideration.

I do not know what may turn up, or what more may be known of the particulars; but at any rate, I am in hopes that the man on whom suspicion rests will be found before very long, and produced at the adjourned inquiry. He is entitled to be present if he turns up, and I should like to give him an opportunity of doing so.'

At this, the inquest was adjourned for a week, and a new venue, the Stag Inn, was decided upon. The only remaining duty on this day was for the body of Arthur Dyson to be formally identified by his wife in the presence of the coroner and Inspector Bradbury, the senior policeman in this area of Sheffield. Sadly, the whole jury were also present at the tragic moment Kate said goodbye to her husband, whose remains were then released for burial.

It is also worth noting that Inspector Bradbury had in his possession a letter from the Home Secretary, in which it was detailed that any assistance in apprehending the suspect would be granted. However, the police were not to apprehend their suspect in time for the re-arranged proceedings; in fact, a description of Peace had been circulated around the entire country during this hiatus, and a generous reward offered for information that would lead to his arrest.

The following day, the body of Arthur Dyson was buried in the churchyard of Ecclesall Church. The day of the funeral had been hastily arranged in order to grant privacy to the grieving family, as a multitude of onlookers had been expected should the date of the funeral have been made public. Just a handful of family members and police officials were in attendance, along with a reporter from the *Sheffield And Rotherham Independent*, who painted a verbose, yet gloomy picture of the events in the following day's edition.

'There was a thick fog settling over the town at noon, and the roads were soaky in the extreme from the heavy showers of rain on the previous night. With an impending shower overhead, this was indeed scant encouragement to remain, but those who had sufficient fortitude to stay lived in hopes of seeing the hearse come up the hill, if only to encourage forward the phlegmatic Sexton to the completion of his task.'

The sense of anger and revulsion in the area was tangible and the bleak weather only served to highlight the dark clouds which had fallen over the community during the previous week. In the light of this, Peace was a hated man, and even the description of him which had been sent to every police station in the country was suitably scathing.

'Charles Peace wanted for murder on the night of the 29th inst. He is thin and slightly built, from fifty-five to sixty years of age. Five feet four inches or five feet high; grey (nearly white) hair, beard and whiskers. He lacks use of three fingers of left hand, walks with his legs rather wide apart, speaks somewhat peculiarly as though his tongue were too large for his mouth, and is a great boaster. He is a picture-frame maker. He occasionally cleans and repairs clocks and watches and sometimes deals in oleographs, engravings and pictures. He has been in penal servitude for burglary in Manchester. He has lived in Manchester, Salford, and Liverpool and Hull.'

However detailed and descriptive this damning portrait of a wanted man may be, it proved to be of no assistance in prompting any response from any members of public who may have come across this distinctive character. And as such, the inquest was opened once again in the absence of a defendant.

At 10am on the morning of 8 December 1874, those who had been so apologetically told to return home a week earlier once again assembled at the new venue to do their duty to the deceased. The first to speak was the widowed Kate Dyson, retelling the tale in a low voice, with her slight Irish brogue barely discernible amidst her personal feelings of loss and sorrow.

She appears to have been treated with great sympathy and tact by Mr Wightman, as she was allowed to recount the events of that fateful night at her own pace, and even when questioned with regard to her previous relationship with Peace, her short and hesitant answers were duly noted and went unquestioned.

She claimed to have known Peace as a neighbour, and admitted to the jury that she had, on occasion, accompanied him to musical events and fairs. She described how their relationship had been one of friendship, and that her husband had also been friendly with Peace at the beginning. However, she was to publically admit that her later meetings with Peace were without the consent of her husband, who had grown tired of the constant presence of his neighbour, and had heard him to be 'a man of very bad character.'

Kate's accounts of the events immediately before the fatal shooting of her husband were exactly as was told to the police in the aftermath of the crime. However, one tiny morsel of intrigue was revealed as she made her closing remarks. When asked if Peace had immediately fled after the shooting, she mentioned a minute detail which is as fascinating as it is inconsequential.

Upon reaching the far side of street, Peace had paused momentarily, and turned to look at the screaming woman and her dying husband. When asked why she believed that an escaping assailant would look back, she answered 'to see if he should fire again I expect.'

The focus of the inquiry then turned to the doctor who attended Arthur Dyson as his life slipped away in the parlour of his new home. Dr J.W. Harrison, a local surgeon who was brought to attend the dying man was one of the key witnesses at the inquest, and as such, described in detail the scene which greeted him on his arrival.

'I was fetched about nine o'clock on the night of the murder to see Mr Dyson. I found him sitting in a chair. He was talking, but was insensible. As he was losing blood fast I had him immediately laid on a mattress, and then examined a wound on the left temple. He never recovered consciousness, and died in my presence at about a quarter to eleven.

Mrs Dyson was present, and also a man named Gregory [ironically, this was the man whom Peace had intended to visit, but had not been at home when he called]. I have since made a post mortem examination, assisted by Mr John Benson. The wound on his left temple was about an inch above the external orbit of the eye, and I could pass a little finger right through it to the skull and into the brain.

The bullet [which Dr Harrison produced] travelled obliquely and took an upward direction. From this latter fact, I imagine that the man who fired the shot was at a lower angle than the deceased. I did not make a sufficiently minute examination to say whether the deceased was a healthy man, because the presence of the bullet in his brain fully accounted for death, and all of the symptoms I saw.'

With the medical evidence being as conclusive as could possibly be in an age where forensic investigation was very much in its infancy, the subject of enquiry then turned to the identity of the man who fired this devastating shot. Many witnesses were present; some who had attended the scene after hearing the shots, and some who clearly remembered their encounter with an unusual and demanding man, shortly before the violent culmination of the evening.

The first of these witnesses to be called was Mrs Sarah Colgrave, who had been accosted in the street by a stranger who had asked her questions about the Dysons and then implored her to take a note to Kate. The woman remembered this unusual request in detail, as this was not the kind of unwarranted conversation that often took place in the streets of Banner Cross.

She recalled a man with grey pointed whiskers who engaged her in conversation as she walked towards the shop owned by (the often mentioned) Mr Gregory. The man asked her if she lived on the street, to which she replied she did not. He then asked her if she knew the *strangers* living at the second house in the row. She replied that she knew of them, but they were not acquaintances.

After this, she recalled the unusual turn of conversation in which the stranger claimed to have 'been intimate' with the lady of the household. She was then asked to call on the Dysons, and deliver a letter to the aforementioned lady of the house. She flatly refused, and went on to say:

'I said he must go himself, and then left him at the lamp a few yards from Mr Gregory's door. He was then walking slowly up, and was a short distance from the Dyson's. I stayed in Gregory's shop about ten minutes, and as I was leaving, I saw him coming out of the passage to Mr Dyson's house, and across the road. He then went up the hill and I never saw him again.'

Mrs Colgrave's account was extremely detailed in her recounting of the conversation which had obviously taken her by surprise. However, it would appear that her knack for recalling physical features was not so accurate, as she was unable to physically describe the man who had so rudely accosted her. The man's grey whiskers, and an approximate age of 45, were the only physical characteristics which had come to mind when remembering this strange event.

Next to testify was the reportedly illiterate labourer, Mr Charles Brassington, who had encountered Peace while standing beneath the gaslight outside the Banner Cross Hotel. This conversation with Brassington seems to have been a bawdier version of that which Peace had earlier embarked upon with Mrs Colgrave, a more man-to-man discussion of Peace's current situation.

Brassington told the inquest that he had seen an 'oldish' man walking backwards and forwards in the immediate vicinity. The man then approached him beneath the lamp and asked him where he lived, and asked if he knew the Dysons. He replied that he did not, and at this, the man pulled from his coat pocket some photographs which he showed to Brassington.

The coroner seems to have been wary of this piece of evidence, and quickly asked whether these photographs were of an 'indecent' nature. Brassington replied that they were not, and that there were three photographs, one of a lone woman, one of a couple, and one of a lone man. However, the witness was unable to identify anyone in the photographs, as he had been keen to show no interest in conversing with the man any longer.

However, one part of the conversation did stick in Brassington's mind. He revealed that upon being asked to read some letters, he advised the stranger that he could not read, before the man made a chilling statement, from which many conclusions can be drawn.

'He caught hold of my sleeve and asked me to read some letters, I told him I could not. He then said that he would make it warm for them before morning, and that he would shoot them both.'

Understandably, this was the point at which Brassington took his leave of the man and his threatening conversation. His physical description of the stranger was similar to that of Mrs Colgrave and his lack of observation was credited to a desire to walk away from the man as soon as possible.

As this was the first time the threat had been mentioned during the course of the investigation, Mr Wightman, the coroner, was keen to press the issue, and record exactly the words that the suspect had spoken. Brassington stated that they were the words as closely as he could recall them, but confirmed that he took the targets of the threat to be Kate and Arthur Dyson.

The line of enquiry then turned to events after the fatal shooting, in which several local residents were alerted to the attack by the sounds of gunshots and screams in the street below their windows. One such witness was Charles Whyman, who had been sitting by the window of the Banner Cross Hotel, enjoying a mug of ale in the warmth of the pub's front room.

Whyman, a quarryman who lived locally, recalled hearing the report of 'a pistol or something', closely followed by another. Along with other drinkers in the pub that evening, he immediately leapt from his seat and through the front door of the pub to investigate. His testimony is very valuable in painting a picture of this terrible scene.

'I was in the front room of the Banner Cross Hotel; it was about half past eight. I was six doors off Mr Dyson's house. There were others in the room. I went to the door and heard a woman squealing "Murder".

I went down to her, it was Mrs Dyson. Mr Dyson was lying on his back on the outside of the entry. Mrs Dyson was holding his head up from the ground. She said "this villain has shot my husband, and he's gone across the road." I did not see him; I went across the road to see if I could see anything of him, but did not.'

The first professional on the scene was Constable Ward, who regularly walked the beat around the Banner Cross Area, and was just a short distance away when the shots were heard. It was Ward who found letters and an envelope, which had been dropped by Peace as he escaped. He described them as being in a roll, but not tied with string.

Constable Ward's first instinct was to trace the steps of the assailant, and as such, it was while striding in the same direction the attacker had fled that he found the letters; he also found some muddy footprints within four or five yards of the letters and found traces of mud where the fugitive had climbed over a garden wall.

The initiative and quick-thinking of this police officer has to be applauded, as these discoveries were made on the opposite side of the street, which had no lighting. It is unfortunate that the suspect had been too quick in fleeing for these signs of escape to be useful in hunting down a killer, but the roll of letters were invaluable to the investigation, especially as one of them was addressed to a *Mr C. Peace Esq.*.

The contents of the tell-tale envelope were even more fascinating, even though its contents amounted to nothing more than a single coin, a coin which would see Kate Dyson once again called back to give further evidence. This was a rarity, especially in 19th century Yorkshire. It was a shiny, American one cent coin.

The police, and anyone who knew the Dysons, were aware that they had spent several years living in Ohio, USA, and coins from the other side of the world were not something which the average chap would have in his possession. However, to a man like Charles Peace, who had a passion for unusual objects, this could have easily been a sentimental gift, given by someone who had travelled to the New World.

However, Kate Dyson vehemently denied having given the coin to her former friend, and when asked if she had ever seen it before, she affirmed that she had seen hundreds of coins like this, having spent years in the United States, and that she had never given a coin of any denomination or origin to Charles Peace.

One can only imagine the embarrassment to Kate Dyson of being called back to the inquest to answer a question which cast this grieving widow in such bad light. Add to this the letters between herself and Peace, which had now become official evidence in the investigation, and this amounts to a woman who would feel very self-conscious in a room full of her neighbours and friends.

It was perhaps fortunate then, at least for Mrs Dyson, that the coroner decided he had heard enough to conclude the inquest. The report of Mr Wightman's summing up is taken from the December 8 late edition of the *Sheffield And Rotherham Independent*.

'The coroner then summed up, he did not intend to call any more evidence, as in all probability the jury would come to a conclusion with that which had been brought before them. As it was, there had been a very full inquiry into the death of the man, Arthur Dyson.

Inspector Bradbury, he was bound to say, had got up the case exceedingly well, and had brought forward apparently every person who knew anything about the matter whose evidence could be of the slightest importance in the inquiry. Indeed, the only thing he had not done, and ought to have done, was to apprehend Peace. He has no doubt, however, that he tried his best to do so.

They were therefore satisfied that the cause of death was the firing of a bullet from a gun or pistol. The question was who fired it, and how came the deceased to be shot. The evidence was really very conclusive, and he did not feel he needed to trouble (the jury) with any remarks about it.

The jury did not wish the evidence to be read for them, in so much as it was very clear, and after deliberation for a few minutes with closed doors, they returned a verdict of WILFUL MURDER against PEACE.'

Chapter 8

One-Armed Jemmy

'Sin goes in a disguise, and thence is welcome; like Judas,
it kisses and kills; like Joab, it salutes and slays.'
George Swinnock, English Puritan, 1627-1673

With his ears still ringing from the ungodly symphony of gunshots and screams, Charlie Peace disappeared into the darkness like an unwelcome gust of icy wind. In his wake he had left a scene of unimaginable terror, yet with the curiosity of a callous killer, he had to look back. He allowed himself this split second of tasteless voyeurism, taking in the scene and committing it to the dark corners of his memory.

A split second was all he needed. The gaslight illuminated the damage he had done, and allowed him one last look into the wide and tearful eyes of the hysterical Kate Dyson. Her screams towards him continued to echo across the icy street, but he had no response to offer. Turning his back and quickening his stride, he fled into the nearby fields until the gaslight could no longer be seen.

Negotiating his way across the frozen ground and the bare tree branches of Endcliffe Woods, Peace fled with all the determination of an already condemned man. He knew that it would be an extremely brave or extremely foolish man who would follow a gunman into such a place in the dead of night, and with his own freedom his foremost concern, he continued deeper into the inhospitable woodland.

Of course, the cover of the woods eventually began to thin, and Peace was left with a dilemma - head straight for the town centre and bide his time until the trains began to run, or keep walking, hoping that a moving target would be more difficult to catch. With a matter of hours before the first trains would pull out of the midland station, he chose to keep walking.

Continuing uphill into the quiet district of Crookes, Peace then made a circuit of the back streets, eventually coming back on himself and reaching the main road. He then decided to head back downhill, towards Broomhill and nearer to the town centre. He had begun to smell the freedom in his lungs and, as a result, made the decision to hail a passing cab.

Although blessed with no shortage of determination and mental strength, physically Peace had his limitations. Having limped his way from the crime scene and across the eastern suburbs of Sheffield, his twisted and gnarled limbs would have been aching, which left him with no option but to risk encountering another human being on the dark, deserted streets.

However, taking a cab in Victorian England was a very different prospect to making the same journey now. The driver would have been seated on top of the carriage, steering his horse, while the passenger sat inside, unseen by the eyes of any people they may have passed at this early hour. There would be no small talk on this cab ride.

His destination was to be Spring Street, where Peace paid the driver, and knocked on the door of a house belonging to a friend. He was a stone's throw from the West Bar police station, yet knew that he had to just wait a few more hours, and this would be much easier behind closed doors. The identity of his friend was never revealed, possibly in an attempt to prevent any future prosecution for aiding a felon.

It was to be in this relatively short space of time that Peace would use his ingenuity to fashion a disguise from nothing. Swapping his clothes for a new outfit provided by his friend was a good start, but it was in this house that Peace first came up with one of his most creative methods of disguise. Using walnut oil, he stained the skin of his hands and face, before once again stepping out into the street.

Looking to all who came across him like a mixed-race gentleman of advancing years, Peace finally felt safe enough to venture into the city centre, but needed to make a quick stop on the way. Calling into the home of his mother (who no doubt was shocked to find a strange mixed-race gentleman banging on her door at the crack of dawn), Peace confessed that he had committed a grave crime, and would be in touch upon reaching safety.

Jane Peace was no stranger to her son's nefarious activities, having stood by him through several arrests and at least four prison sentences; but to hear that her own son was a murderous fugitive may have been a severe shock to the system, as poor Mrs Peace begged her son to take his leave and get as far away from the family as possible.

Adhering to his mother's wishes, Peace headed out into the sunrise and made his way, not to the main midland station, but to Attercliffe station, just a short walk away. Here, he would be less likely to be noticed, as this was a small, unmanned station with just two platforms, one heading back to Sheffield, and the other towards neighbouring Rotherham.

Heading out of Sheffield and its outlying districts, Peace reached the main station in Rotherham, and again chose to take an alternative route on the next part of his journey, walking through the town centre to the district of Masborough, and the much smaller station in this neighbourhood. It was from here that Peace could safely make his escape from South Yorkshire.

His destination was Beverley, a town in North Yorkshire, from where he could easily travel to Hull, his second home, and the current home of his family. Knowing that his time at home would be fleeting, Peace set about improving his disguise, which was perhaps unnecessary after his own daughter had failed to recognise him as he approached the house!

Ever the inventor, Peace at least had tools at his disposal upon reaching the eating house which he had bought as a family business, and wasted no time in manufacturing the pièce de résistance of his already convincing disguise. He could change his colouring and his dress style, even conceal his limp if required, but concealing the missing finger of his left hand would take a much more cunning invention.

Replacing a lost digit would be impossible, but losing an entire hand was a feasible option. With this in mind, Peace began work on one of the most impressive props he would ever create. He created a tube from gutta percha (a type of Malaysian tree sap which was a forerunner to plastic, and an alternative to expensive rubber) into which he was able to insert his entire left hand and forearm.

Fixing a hook to the end of the tube, Peace was now able to pass himself off as a man who had lost his entire hand, and wore a prosthetic, rather than a man with a missing finger. This, combined with his change in dress style, and alteration of his skin tone, had served to create an entirely new man, a man who could walk the streets unhindered by fear of apprehension.

His new dress style was one of a respectable gentleman, a dark suit and gold-rimmed spectacles worked wonders in concealing the dangerous criminal beneath, and as an extra facet to his new appearance, Peace could also employ some unique talents at a moment's notice, being blessed with an ability to become unrecognisable at the merest sign of trouble.

A broken jaw sustained some years before had left Peace with the grotesque ability to dislocate it at will, which gave him a protruding chin and pronounced under-bite. Another strange technique used by Peace was a unique way of allowing the blood to rush to his head (presumably by clenching his afflicted jaw) which provided him a natural way of altering his skin tone on the spot.

Despite this arrangement, Peace continued to apply walnut oil to his skin in order to darken his tone, and applied dye to his thinning prematurely-grey hair. As detailed as the description of him that had been circulated around the nation by this point was, it would take an eagle-eye of extraordinary vigilance to identify the dark-haired, mixed-race businessman as Charles Frederick Peace.

Happy with his new identity, but still harbouring a fear of apprehension, Peace soon said goodbye to his family, and would spend the last days of 1876, and the first week of 1877, travelling the country in a deliberately random manner, zig-zagging from county to county, and surviving on the proceeds of a string of low-profile burglaries committed during his travels.

In a brave move, Peace had first headed back into South Yorkshire, but spent only hours in the county of his birth, taking a train from Doncaster to King's Cross, before heading to the distant anonymity of Bristol, and then to Bath, all the time looking over his shoulder to ensure that he was not being followed.

It would appear that, by the time Peace left Bath on a train to Oxford, his fears of being caught had given way to his old sense of callous bravado, as he deliberately decided to test out his new disguise in the most brazen manner possible. If he could survive this train journey, he could survive anything.

ONE-ARMED JEMMY

Taking a seat directly opposite a uniformed policeman, Peace began to make conversation with the sergeant, politely enquiring as to his business on a train to Oxford. At this, the policeman nodded to the woman who accompanied him, informing Peace that he had been asked to accompany the woman to court, as she had been charged with stealing £40 from her employers.

His callousness knowing no end, this well dressed gentleman took it upon himself to deliver a lecture to the young woman, warning her of the spiritual ruin which would be heaped upon her if she continued her immoral ways. At no point did the policeman show even a spark of recognition, even when in deep conversation with Britain's most wanted man.

In later days, Peace would describe the young sergeant as 'a smart chap, but not smart enough to know me!' However, given the extent of his elaborate disguise, one would suspect that even a high-ranking detective would have been fooled by the talkative stranger who had delivered such a thorough and righteous lecture to his prisoner.

Upon reaching Oxford, Peace again moved quickly, heading for Birmingham where he stayed for a week, before travelling to Derby. It was a matter of days before he moved on again, this time ending his journey for the foreseeable future in Nottingham. The date was 9 January 1877, and Peace was about to begin a new life in the Midlands.

Just short of six weeks since his escape into the darkness of Banner Cross, Peace had travelled the country in a loop, before ending up just 45 miles from his hometown and the scene of his terrible crime. This had been his plan all along. The police would search the far corners of the nation for him, but would fail to look closer to home.

True to his humble roots, and with the continuation of his criminal career in mind, Peace immediately headed for Nottingham's poorer areas; it was here that he found himself once again amongst the criminal gangs and questionable establishments. This was the kind of life that he had chosen for himself and this was where he could lose himself in the crowds.

The area to which Peace was drawn was known colloquially as the Marsh, covering the districts of the disreputable Broad Marsh and the downright dangerous Narrow Marsh. These were districts largely avoided by the police, given their fearsome reputations and close knit communities. Although the residents of the Marsh were generally suspicious of strangers, this was to be an area where Peace would fit in like a true native.

Narrow Marsh in particular was a teeming warren of slum housing and filthy streets and it was here that Peace immediately took lodgings among a local population, most of whom had no wish to live by the laws of the land. This was the ideal place to spend his days in safety, before travelling into the more affluent areas of Nottingham by night.

The lowly lodgings he had found were at the house of a Mrs Adamson, who was well known in the Marsh as an expert receiver of stolen goods, hawking ill-gotten gains in the pawn shops of the city, and laundering the proceeds with much more success than she would ever have in laundering the lice-infested bed linen of her lodging house.

The following weeks were spent engaging in petty theft in order to pay for his lodgings, and Peace soon became known to the criminal elements of the Marsh, and was readily accepted as one of them, especially by the young urchins who made their livings by picking pockets and shoplifting and to whom Peace became known affectionately as One-armed Jemmy.

Life in Nottingham could not have been developing any better for the newly arrived Jemmy, as his illegally gained profits could be handed immediately to his landlady, who would then subtract his rent money from the profits, and hand him back the remainder (minus a fee, of course). It was an arrangement that both parties were happy with.

It was in the home of Mrs Adamson, and during the surreptitious passing of a stolen box of cigars, that Peace would meet the woman who was to become his new obsession. As Mrs Adamson haggled for her 30 per cent, Peace was immediately captivated by the woman who watched the sordid proceedings with interest. Her name was Susan Gray.

Although just twelve years younger than Peace, Susan Gray could have easily passed for his daughter; a fact which speaks volumes with regards to her youthful appearance, and his gnarled and wretched features. She was also well educated, an attribute which was immediately appreciated by the worldly Peace, and had previously been a music hall singer, known locally as 'the Nottingham Nightingale.'

This ex-songbird had been, and in the eyes of law still was, married to a man named Bailey who had grown tired of his wife for reasons which were as yet unknown to Peace, although her husband did still provide her with a weekly allowance. So taken was Peace by Susan Gray, that he spent the rest of the day brooding on this momentous meeting and set his sights upon the new target of his desires.

That evening was to be an eventful one as Peace continued his brooding over a bottle of cheap Irish whiskey. Before long, and with his fears of capture gone like the contents of the whiskey bottle, Peace headed out into the street, shouting into the night air that he would shoot the woman who had become his infatuation if he could not have her.

No doubt annoyed by the shouting and drunkenness, Mrs Adamson sent for Susan Gray to come to the lodging house and calm her troublesome resident. Surprisingly, she immediately came to the house to aid a drunken man who had threatened to shoot her. Peace was immediately pacified at the sight of his intended conquest, and after a brief conversation in which Gray assured him that she would like to see him again; peace was once again restored to the Marsh.

Racked with guilt, and probably a terrible hangover, Peace again sent for Susan the following morning and offered his sincere apologies as to his behaviour the previous evening. His emotional outpourings had been enough to convince her that he was genuinely besotted, and from that day forward she became the mistress of a murderous fugitive.

Keen to throw off the past, Gray decided to rid herself of both her maiden name and her married name, and began to refer to herself as Mrs Thompson. It would appear that Peace wasn't the only party in this relationship keen to cover up the past and before long it was time for Peace to reveal the true extent of his criminal past. After all, he didn't want his new mistress to think of him as just a small time burglar.

Undeterred by his confessions, Susan vowed to keep his secret and in return was the recipient of gifts and a fine lifestyle funded by the ever escalating burglaries committed by Peace, as he quickly moved away from petty theft to his particular area of expertise, the breaking and entering of affluent households.

His renewed career was gaining momentum, until one fateful day, when the master burglar was spotted as he attempted to steal some fine linen from a wealthy home. As had become his custom, he drew his revolver towards the witness, but this time there were to be no shots fired, and Peace was able to escape back to the slums of Narrow Marsh.

Angry at himself and worried that he had been identified, Peace immediately sent for Susan, and told her to quickly prepare for a trip. Unfortunately for Susan, this was to be no romantic break; the destination was Hull, home to Peace's family and his resilient and long-suffering wife, Hannah. One can only imagine that this was not a factor listed by Peace when convincing his mistress to accompany him.

With the breathtaking brazenness that only Peace could dream of, he found lodgings in Hull for himself and his 'wife' with a policeman and his family. Having introduced himself as a businessman, and with both Peace and Susan wearing their finest clothing, the constable had immediately taken his guests at their word, and was only too happy to rent out his spare room to this seemingly well-to-do couple.

Keeping a low profile was something which did not come naturally to Charlie Peace, and with his mistress otherwise occupied, he decided to pay a visit to his family, but not before ensuring that he would not be recognised. This was a staggering act of boldness, one which left even his own family, who were more than used to his eccentricities, dumbfounded.

Peace was smart enough to stay away from the premises he owned along with his family, as he suspected that the eating house was under surveillance by the police, and instead wrote a short note in pencil, which he paid a passing child a few pennies to deliver into the hands of his common-law wife. The note read *"I am waiting to see you. Just up Anlaby Road."*

Although well aware that her husband had disguised himself in the aftermath of Arthur Dyson's murder, nothing could prepare Hannah Peace, and her stepson, Wiilie, for the sight that greeted them on their arrival. This was a person who bore no resemblance to the man who had left Hull covered in walnut oil and sporting a homemade prosthetic.

Charles Peace stood resplendent in a tailored black suit, top hat, and velvet waistcoat. This astonishing new image was accompanied by a gold-topped walking cane, suede gloves, and a small yapping dog which ran circles around his well-shod feet as he stood. If his family had not known better, they would have assumed that they were in the presence of a wealthy and well connected gentleman.

One can only imagine the conversation which took place between man and wife on this street corner, but what is known, is that Peace informed his wife of his current lodgings, but failed to mention the woman with whom he shared them. Vowing to return one day and take his place amongst his family, Peace explained that he could not stay long, as he was fearful of being spotted, although his current attire would certainly make any positive identification of him extremely difficult.

In the weeks that passed, Peace returned to his burglaries with remarkable success; he still had the skills and daring for this work and his ever-growing wealth reflected this. However, it would transpire that his activities were too successful. Dining with the policeman who rented out his room to Peace one night, conversation turned to the string of sensational burglaries which had recently been experienced by the wealthy and influential citizens of Hull.

Peace had not been recognised, but his handiwork certainly had been. It would not be long before the authorities would put two and two together, and realise that a master criminal was at work, a master criminal who had family ties in Hull. It was time for another move, and another farewell to the East Riding of Yorkshire.

By the time Peace and Susan Gray heaved the last of their luggage onto a train back to Nottingham, the shop windows of Hull were already beginning to display posters offering a reward of £50 for information leading to the capture of Britain's most wanted man, although luckily for Peace, his description had not been changed since his escape from the law in Sheffield.

However, on returning to the Marsh, Peace found that it wasn't long before the wanted posters had made their way down to the Midlands. Unable to resist a few more burglaries to tide the couple over, and pay Mrs Adamson the rent owed, the couple gambled on staying in Nottingham for just a short while; but it was to be a short stay which almost led to the downfall of Charlie Peace.

Whilst lying in bed with his mistress one day, Peace was rudely disturbed by two detectives bursting into the room and demanding to know the identity of the furious man beneath the bedclothes. It would appear that Susan Gray (or Thompson) was already known to the police, as they addressed her as Mrs Bailey, and expressed shock that she should be caught in such a situation with a man that certainly wasn't Mr Bailey.

Peace controlled his rage enough to falsely introduce himself as John Ward (the name by which Susan Gray would always refer to him), a travelling spectacle salesman from Hull. Mortified by the thought that someone (possibly Mrs Adamson) had reported his true identity to the police, Peace humbly asked that he may be allowed to dress in private before meeting with the two detectives downstairs. Surprisingly, this request was granted and the policemen left the room accompanied by Susan Gray.

What followed was another momentous event in the criminal career of Charlie Peace. Dressing hurriedly and opening the upstairs window, Peace leapt from the windowsill landing on an adjacent outhouse, and running as fast as his limp would allow him, heading into the warren of narrow streets which surrounded the lodging house.

On hearing the sound of Peace landing heavily on the roof of the outhouse, the two detectives had sprung from their seats to investigate, only to find an open window and a grubby pair of net curtains billowing in the breeze. Their suspect had gone, running for his life into the teeming alleyways and conveniently adjoining yards of the Marsh.

A warning was immediately put out across the whole of the Nottinghamshire police that a suspected killer was on the loose somewhere within the city, but due to the primitive communication methods available to the authorities in Victorian England, the suspect was never located. It was as if he had vanished into the walls of the city.

To her great relief, Susan Gray had received a message just hours after the daring escape, instructing her to join him in a distant suburb of Nottingham. Ever obedient to her lover, Susan immediately followed, taking care to ensure that she was not followed. This was to be the true test of her dedication to Peace, and it was a test that she passed with flying colours.

By the time the police had been briefed that Peace might be in the area, this well-dressed and seemingly respectable couple had already boarded a train, along with a few pieces of essential luggage. Looking every inch the genteel couple without a care in the world, the two settled into their seats for the long journey south.

Their destination was to be London, which at that time was the largest and most populous city in the world. This would be the ideal place to shed their identities once more, and start a new life in a city which promised a wealth of opportunity and a greater chance of anonymity.

Chapter 9

Bullets Fly in Blackheath

'I like the spirit of this great London which I feel around me.
Who but a coward would pass his whole life in hamlets; and
forever abandon his faculties to the eating rust of obscurity?'
Charlotte Brontë, Novelist and Poet, 1816-1855

Victorian London had everything a man of Charlie Peace's situation and tastes could possibly desire. It was the epicentre of an Empire, and as such, could boast a wealth of cultural riches and endless possibilities. For a man with a love of music and art, and a tireless sense of adventure, this was as close as a wicked murderer could ever come to finding heaven.

Yet beyond the imposing towers and majestic architecture lay a sprawling land of poverty and crime. Such was the extent of this lawless sub-city that a man could easily lose himself within the heaving crowds of common folk struggling their way through life. It was in the grand galleries and countless concert halls that Peace could enjoy life in the nation's capital, but it was in these narrow, fetid streets that he would initially ply his immoral trades.

The London district of Lambeth has been in existence for almost a millennium, having been recorded for posterity in written documents since 1062, when the area was known as *Lambehitha*, meaning "landing place of the lambs". However, its newest resident was anything but a lamb; he was a lion let loose in the streets of the parish.

By 1877, the area had become something of an embarrassment to its former self. Gone were the tranquil farmlands fed by the mighty River Thames, only to be replaced by a maze of dirty streets, winding their way through the borough like diseased arteries, carrying a steady flow of crime and poverty towards the banks of the famous river.

These unwelcoming streets were home to a large number of

workhouses and cheap lodgings, brought into existence by the unstoppable flow of economic migrants heading to the city with dreams of wealth and success, only to find the stinking inner-city suburbs filled with the effects of poverty. This was exactly the type of place that Charlie Peace was drawn to, knowing that he could thrive in the mean streets and could make a living by any means possible.

Immediately settling in the inauspicious surroundings of 25 Stangate Street, which has since been engulfed into the developing area of Upper Marsh, Peace had found the perfect place for himself and Susan. The poverty and lawlessness of the area made it possible to live in relative safety and anonymity from the authorities, but just a few minutes across the Thames was the centre of the Empire: Westminster.

Peace was living in the belly of the beast, right under the nose of the same government which had offered such a hefty reward for his capture, but was hidden from sight, as was every resident of the London slums, by the squeamishness of those in power when it came to recognising the poor and needy that shared the city with the rich and royalty.

Still presenting an image that marked him as a respectable and trustworthy individual (although the top hat, cane and kid gloves had since been dispensed with), Peace frequently walked the streets of Lambeth dressed in a dark, modest suit and gold-rimmed spectacles. He was the epitome of the working-class businessman, ambitious and energetic, yet without the breeding to see him living on the other side of the Thames.

Keen to establish a legitimate business, Peace set himself up as a trader of musical instruments which he bought and sold from his lodgings in Stangate Street. The couple quickly became popular amongst the other residents of Lambeth, owing to Susan's friendly and outgoing nature and Peace's eccentricity and musical talent. For once, it seemed to the couple that they had found their place in the world, and only the revelation of their terrible secrets could damage this new-found happiness.

Known to all who frequented their home as Mr and Mrs Thompson, the two frequent travellers seemed to have put away their suitcases for the foreseeable future. The musical instrument business was doing well enough to put food on the table and take care of the modest rent but, as always with Charlie Peace, a modest income was never enough.

Most of the musical instruments in Peace's home had uncertain origins, with no records of any kind kept as to the details of his trading. In fact, had any musician from a neighbouring area visited Peace in order to replace a missing instrument, it was more than likely that they would return home having paid for the missing item, albeit a polished and slightly altered version of its former self.

Peace had always been a man who could not help himself when it came to helping himself, and it wasn't long after their arrival in Lambeth that he would slip away into Camberwell or other neighbouring districts under cover of darkness and return home with his pony pulling a cart full of new stock for his business.

The acquisition of the pony, named 'Tommy' by his new owner, had been the first piece of business attended to by 'Mr Thompson' after securing lodgings for himself and his 'wife'. Such was his love for animals and talent in taming even the wildest beast (a talent inherited from his father), Peace doted on Tommy, taking more care of the animal than he had ever taken over his now estranged family who languished in Hull, struggling to make ends meet.

It was a match made in heaven; Peace would always find a cathartic pleasure in the wellbeing of Tommy, spending hours every day grooming and feeding his new steed. In return, Tommy would gladly walk the cobbles of London in the early hours, pulling behind him a small cart, usually stuffed with the proceeds of a successful burglary.

Unlike the previous year, the Christmas of 1877 found Peace in good cheer; no longer was he alone, flitting from town to town to preserve his freedom, but he was living a life full of far more joy than he could have ever hoped for, taking the events of the previous year into account. It was in this spirit of festive happiness that Peace finally took the time to reach out to his estranged family, inviting his seventeen year old daughter and her fiancé to join himself and Susan in London.

The invitation was accepted, yet the written response received by Peace from his daughter, Jane, was also to bring sad news. Her namesake, Peace's mother, had passed away in Sheffield some months before. The flying visit just hours after the murder of Arthur Dyson was the last time the two would ever see each other and it was with this sense of regret that Peace decided to keep his loved ones near.

The visit was a pleasant one, with Jane and her betrothed, a collier by

A photograph of Angel Street, Sheffield taken in 1893. The Peace family home in Angel Court was located to the rear of the shops. *Courtesy of sfbhistory.org.uk*

A copy of the 1841 census which confirms the occupants of the Peace family home. *Courtesy of ancestry.co.uk*

A photographic portrait of Charlie Peace during one of his rare periods of freedom.
Courtesy of sheffield history.co.uk

A photographic portrait of Peace taken during his thirties. The life of crime in which he was embroiled had certainly taken its toll.
Courtesy of niha.org.uk

The Britannia Pub, in which Peace would perform to the evening drinkers, often accompanied by Kate Dyson. *Photograph by Ben W. Johnson.*

BURIALS in the Parish of _Chorlton cum Hardy_ in the County of _Lancaster_ in the year One thousand eight hundred and _Seventy Six._

Name.	Abode.	When buried.	Age.	By whom the Ceremony was performed.
Edith Pritchard No. 25	Chorlton cum Hardy	July 26	6 ms.	J. Booth
George Henry Francis No. 26	Stretford	August 3	10 weeks	J. J. Booth
Nicholas Cock No. 27	Chorlton cum Hardy	August 5	22 yrs.	J. J. Booth

A copy of the burial certificate issued after the funeral of PC Nicholas Cock in Greater Manchester. *Courtesy of ancestry.co.uk*

RETURN of all Persons Committed, or Bailed to appear for Trial, or Indicted at the _Afsizes_ ——— held at _Manchester_

on the _23rd_ day of _November_ 1876, shewing the nature of their Offences, and the result of the Proceedings.

No.	NAMES	Offences of which those tried were Convicted or Acquitted, and of which those discharged without Trial were charged on Indictment or Circumstances	Convicted and Sentenced					Acquitted and Discharged
			Death	Penal Servitude	Imprisonment; (state if also Whipped or Fined)	Term of Police Supervision		
1	William Habron	Murder	✱ Death, and his body to be buried within the precincts of the Prison					
2	William Flannagan, alias William Robinson	Murder	Death, and his body to be buried within the precincts of the Prison					
3	~~James Vaughan~~	~~Murder~~	~~Death and his body to be buried within the precincts of the Prison~~					✗
4	George Jackson	Manslaughter (Indicted for Murder)	✓ 10 Years					
5	Thomas Taylor	Carnally knowing and abusing a Girl under the age of twelve years	✓ 10 Years					
6	William Stanley	Burglary before convicted of Felony	✓ 10 Years					
7	Ebenezer Wareing	Burglary	✓ 10 Years					
8	Robert Riley	Bestiality	✓ 10 Years					
9	James Kelly	Burglary before convicted of Felony	✓ 7 Years					
	James Clegg (on two Indictments)							
10	Cornelius Crowther	Burglary before convicted of Felony	✓ 7 Years					
11	John Walker	Forging Acceptances of Bills of Exchange and Uttering the same, knowing them to be forged (on two Indictments) and Embezzlement (on another Indictment)	✓ 7 Years					
12	John Smith	Burglary before convicted of Felony (on two Indictments) (From North Lancashire)	✓ 7 Years					
13	James Bown	Wounding with intent to do grievous bodily harm	✓ 5 Years					
14	John William Pearson	Wounding with intent to do grievous bodily harm	✓ 5 Years					
15	Michael Ruth	Unlawfully Wounding	✓ 5 Years					
16	Joseph Clegg	Manslaughter	✓ 5 Years					
17	Joseph Baxter	Rape	✓ 5 Years					
18	Thomas Gregory	Forging an Order for the delivery of Goods and uttering the same, knowing it to be forged	✓ 5 Years					
19	James Spence	Obtaining Money by false pretences	✓ 5 Years					
20	~~William McGee~~		5 Years					✗
21	Joseph Norris	Forging an Order for the payment of Money and Uttering the same, knowing it to be forged (on two another Indictments) Obtaining Money by false pretences			✓ 18 Months			
22	William Rhodes	Attempt to Murder			✓ 15 Months			
23	James Cox	Burglary before convicted of Felony			✓ 15 Months			
24	John Adolph Clewarth	Forging a Receipt for Money and Uttering the same, knowing it to be forged and (on another Indictment) Falsifying Accounts			✓ 15 Months			
25	Robert Grundy	Manslaughter			✓ 15 Months			
26	Charles Whalley	Rape			✓ 15 Months			
27	Thomas Turney	Rape			✓ 15 Months			
28	Daniel Helton	Maliciously damaging Machinery prepared for spinning of cotton with intent to render the same useless			✓ 12 Months			
29	William Bow	Burglary			✓ 12 Months			
30	John Haughton	Robbery with violence			✓ 12 Months			

Home Office Return.   It is requested that where more than one Sheet is used, each may bear a separate Heading, as the Returns are bound up as Records.

28 —

The sentence cruelly handed down to young William Habron, which was thankfully commuted to life imprisonment before his eventual pardon. *Courtesy of ancestry.co.uk*

The grave of PC Nicholas Cock, his headstone is now located at Lancashire Police HQ. *Courtesy of Google Images.*

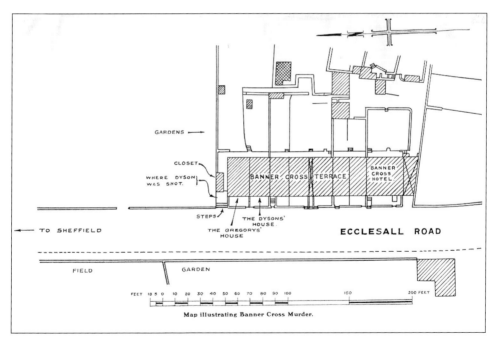

A diagram of the Banner Cross Terrace crime scene. *Courtesy of sheffieldhistory.co.uk*

The Banner Cross Hotel in which Peace was drinking before the murder of Arthur Dyson, just a few yards away from the crime scene. *Photograph by Ben W. Johnson.*

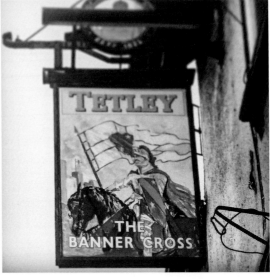

The historic pub sign of the Banner Cross Hotel. *Photograph by Ben W. Johnson.*

Modern day Attercliffe train station. The platform from which Peace embarked upon his escape following the murder of Arthur Dyson. *Photograph by Ben W. Johnson.*

The grave of the unfortunate Arthur Dyson, who was buried in Ecclesall Churchyard. *Courtesy of sheffieldhistory.co.uk*

Ecclesall Church, in which the sombre funeral of Arthur Dyson was held.
Photograph by Ben W. Johnson.

A photograph of 5 East Terrace, Peckham, where Peace lived along with Susan Gray. The basement in which Hannah Peace and Willie Haines lived is visible. *Courtesy of sheffield history.co.uk*

A sketch of PC Edward Robinson, the man who ended Peace's criminal career. *Courtesy of winteringham.info*

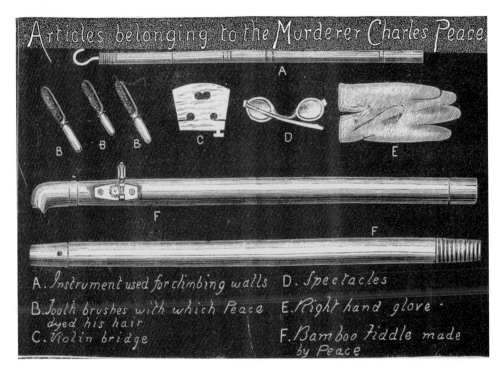

An illustration of the possessions which were found upon the person of Charles Peace during his arrest. *Courtesy of sheffieldhistory.co.uk*

An image of Peace demonstrating his unique talent for disguise. In this image, he has dislocated his jaw in order to alter his appearance.
Courtesy of findagrave.com

Central Criminal Court

Return of all Persons Committed, or Bailed to appear for Trial, or Indicted at the *Sessions* _____ held at *the Old Bailey* on the 18th day of *November* — 1878, showing the nature of their Offences, and the result of the Proceedings.

NAMES	Offence of which these tried were Convicted or Acquitted, and of which those discharged without Trial were charged on Information or Commitment	Convicted and Sentenced				Acquitted and Discharged
		Death	Penal Servitude	Imprisonment ; (state if also Whipped or Fined)	Term of Police Supervision	
... Ward alias Charles Peace	Feloniously shooting to murder	Life				
...ge Roberts	House breaking			18 cal mos		
...jamin Benjamin	Receiving stolen goods					
...omas McCarthy	Burglary			15 cal mos		
...ry Mercer	Larceny & former conv. (common law)			12 cal mos from 21 October		
...m George Seth	Larceny in dwelling house to val £5					
...bert Seth	do do do			9 cal mos		
...t Crawley	Unlawful wounding			3 cal mos		
...ph Steward	Assault	Fined £5 & recogs to keep the Peace for 12 cal mos				
...ph Samuel Mitchell	do	do do do do				

Henry Goode
Clerk of the said Court

9—1

The court document produced during Peace's trial at the Old Bailey for the attempted murder of PC Robinson. *Courtesy of ancestry.co.uk*

County of *Yorkshire West Riding Division*

Returns of all Persons Committed, or Bailed to appear for Trial, or Indicted at the *Winter Assizes 1879* held at *Leeds*

on the *28th* day of *January* 187*9*, shewing the nature of their Offences, and the result of the Proceedings.

No.	NAMES	Offence of which those tried were Convicted or Acquitted, and of which those discharged without Trial were charged on Indictment or Commitment	Convicted and Sentenced				Acquitted and Discharged
			Death	Penal Servitude	Imprisonment: (with if also Whipped or Fined)	Term of Police Supervision	
31	Margaret Bowker	Embezzlement of money whilst in the service of the Post Office		5 years			
32	Edward Allen	Burglary before convicted of felonies		10 years			
33	James Binns	Robbery with violence					Not Guilty
34	James Dyson	Rape		5 years			
35	Charles Gomersall	Larceny of a Post Letter whilst employed in the Post Office			15 Cal. months		
36	George Hales	Manslaughter			3 Cal. months		
37	John McGreavy	Manslaughter					Bill of Indictment not found
38	Jane Hovey	Manslaughter					Bill of Indictment not found
39	Chrs. Peace	Murder	To be hanged				
40	George Monks	Wounding with intent to do grievous bodily harm before Convicted of felonies		5 years			
41	Robt Wormesley Connor	Forgery					Bill of Indictment not found
42	Arthur Laycock	Offences under the Ditties Act 1869					Not Guilty

Edward Bromley
Clerk of Assize

Home Office Return. It is requested that where more than one Sheet is used, each may bear a separate Heading, as the Returns are bound up as Records.

10 — 2

A copy of the court document from Leeds Assizes in which Peace is sentenced to death for the murder of Arthur Dyson. *Courtesy of ancestry.co.uk*

A portrait of William Marwood, the hangman who instigated the use of 'the long drop' in Great Britain, and sent Charlie Peace to meet his maker by this very method.
Courtesy of oldpolicecellsmuseum.org.uk

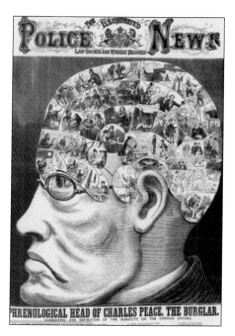

PHRENOLOGICAL HEAD OF CHARLES PEACE, THE BURGLAR.

The front cover of the *Illustrated Police News*, in which a cartoon exploring the extraordinary mind of Charlie Peace is given pride of place.
Courtesy of dailymail.co.uk

A NEW SONG ON

The Trial and Sentence
OF

PEACE,

For the Murder of Mr. Arthur Dyson,
at Bannercross Sheffield, Nov. 29, 76.

Charles Peace, the Blackheath burglar is sentenced now
   to die,
For Mr. Dyson's murder long ago,
He has been wild and reckless, but his day it has gone
   by,
For in the grave he'll soon be lying low.
He has led an evil life, of robbery and strife,
   But his days are numbered in this world
The only friend that's left him is that poor neglected
   wife
Now in the depths of misery she's hurled.

CHORUS.

In heavy irons lying he is condemned to die,
   Charles Peace, the murderer, none can save,
Broken down and dejected his wild career's gone by
   His crimes will soon be ended in the grave

Of all the bold highwaymen in the history of the land,
   He never had an equal in his time,
The riches of the wealthy he stole with cunning hand,
   He has been the terror of those modern times,
He feared no living foe, with his pistol he would go,
   Determined to escape or to die,
The life of Peace the burglar I'm sure will plainly show
   That from justice he could not always fly.

For nearly fifty years he has pursued a life of crime,
   Such as no one ever knew before,
Confined within a prison he has been many times,
   But still he always would defy the law.
Tho' guilty he has been, by many it has been seen,
   True affection sometimes he could show,
He loved his pictures and his birds, they were a joy to
   him
   And his pony loved its master as we know.

He shot poor Mr. Dyson there cannot be a doubt,
   There's no excuse for murder you will say
Mrs. Dyson he pretended he could not live without
   But he'd no right to take her husband's life away.
Every crime beneath the sun perhaps he may have done,
   But if with blood he had not stained his hand,
He may have passed the last few days his life had to run
   In preparing for a better land.

He has fought for life many times, especially on the
   line,
   Although he's getting old and full of years,
If upon the scaffold his life he must resign,
   There's sure to be a friend to drop a tear.
The poor he did befriend, and money he would spend,
   In helping those around him who were poor,
Altho' the laws of England we know he did offend,
   Many things untrue have been said at his door.

His days will soon be over, the hangman soon will come
   The body of the murderer to demand,
To suffer for the many crimes that often he had done,
   Against the peace and welfare of the land,
His doom will teach us all that guilt will have a fall,
   We cannot escape the convict's fate,
When once a crimes committed it is beyond recall,
   And repentance perhaps may come for us too late.

A Victorian music hall song, in which the life and death of Charlie Peace are given the full theatre treatment.
Courtesy of sheffieldhistory.co.uk

WILLIAM HABRON

Sentenced to Death, Augt, 1876, for the Murder of P, C, Cock, at Whalley Range near Manchester. Repreived and sent to Penal Servitude for life, September in the same year. Discovered to be innocent, and Released March 18th, 1879.

Tune:—Teddy O Neal.

I am a poor lad that's seen trouble and sorrow,
But my only crime has been that I was poor,
Upon my young brow there is many a furrow,
Caused by the misery I've had to endure,
Punished for a crime I had no hand in,
I was at one time, sentenced to die,
On the brink of the grave for weeks I was standing
Fully expecting my last hour was nigh.

CHORUS.

My prayer is answer'd cried poor Willm, Habron
God know's how I've suffered for two years & more
Condemned in prison, my lot was a sad one,
But now I am free upon Erin's green share.

I said on the day I was tried for the murder,
I never done harm to a soul in the world,
That cruel day broke the heart of my father,
His poor Irish Boy was in misery hurled,
My blessings be with them who saved me from dying.
A terrible death on the dread gallows tree,
Altho' I was poor I cannot be denying,
Kind hearts in England were thinking of me.

In the prison at Millbank waking or sleeping,
My thoughts were of home, my father and all
I pray'd that the angels a watch would be keeping
On the innocent boy, in those cold cheerless walls,
For I had done nothing the thought it was fearful
To be like a convict, in misery hurled,

The good name I prized they ever took from me
A prison for life I was dead to the world,

May God's blessing rest on my noble Master,
Who spared neither time nor expence in my cause,
When he thought of poor Habron, his kind heart beat faster,
He knew that I had been betrayed by the laws
But he could not tell my heart-broken feeling,
As I went to my slavery day after day,
The quarries at Portland, my young heart was stealing,
My two brightest years they have taken away

The day I was pardoned I rose in the morning,
My Gaolers they call'd me but little I knew,
The hour I pray'd for, at last was just dawning,
And all I had said was found out to be true,
I silently thanked the angels above me,
And bless' those who tried the poor boy to save
I am now in the world among them that love me
Honestly rescued, from that living grave.

Goverment I'm told have made preparations,
For making some compensation to me,
But I would give up all the wealth in the nation
If every innocent Irishman they would set free
They may give me riches but Oh! I would rather
They had left me alone as I worked for my bread
Money will never bring back my poor father
At home in dear Ireland, he is with the dead

F. Jones, Printer, 55, Lambert St. Sheffield.

Another music hall song produced in the aftermath of Peace's execution. This time, the subject of the piece is the unfortunate William Habron. *Courtesy of sheffieldhistory.co.uk*

The legend of Charlie Peace carried on for many years after his execution, with this violent murderer being immortalised in the pages of the penny dreadfuls. *Courtesy of comicsuk.co.uk*

The ultimate honour? Or the ultimate insult? Peace's wax effigy, which was displayed in Madame Tussauds alongside an effigy of William Marwood.
Courtesy of oldpolicecellsmuseum.org.uk

A still from the 1905 short film 'The Life of Charlie Peace', written and filmed by William Haggar, pioneer of the British cinema industry. *Courtesy of williamhaggar.co.uk*

A modern day photograph of Banner Cross Terrace. The scene of the crime was built over in the 1950s and is now the unit marked as 'To Let'. The craft shop was the home of Mr Gregory, and the estate agent now occupies what was the Dyson home.
Courtesy of Google Images.

the name of Bolsover, being taken around London to visit the sights by an impeccably dressed and unusually polite Peace. It was even noted later by Jane Peace that her father approached policemen on a regular basis, politely asking directions and making friendly conversation.

The current living arrangements of her father was something of a tacit subject during this visit for Jane Peace, as to see her father living in relative luxury whilst her mother struggled to provide for herself in Hull was difficult to accept. However, to spend time with her father was a rare opportunity for Jane, although not one that she was prepared to conceal from her long-suffering mother.

By the end of the visit, Bolsover took the opportunity to ask Peace for permission to marry his daughter, a request which was happily granted. Peace had found the young man to be industrious and intelligent, which, along with his cheery disposition, had endeared this young collier to his soon-to-be father-in-law from the moment they met.

However, Peace had no intention of bidding another goodbye to his family, and as soon as the couple returned home to Hull, they found a letter addressed to the whole family waiting for them. In it, Peace had written of his affection and undying love for each of them, and asked that they join himself and Susan in London on a permanent basis, such was the comfortable lifestyle they now enjoyed in the nation's capital.

One can only imagine the reaction of Susan Gray and Hannah Peace to this breathtakingly ambitious attempt to unite his loved ones. However, this new invitation was also accepted. While it does appear that Hannah Peace had made a very bad decision, it must be remembered that life in Hull was increasingly hard for her, working to maintain the eating house which Peace had bought, and without her husband to contribute.

Susan had been pacified by the promise that she would remain the only object of Peace's affections, and that he had made this strange request only in order to provide for his family, who were deserving of their share of his new found success. Begrudgingly, his new partner agreed to his unexpectedly philanthropic idea.

Jane and her fiancé chose not to relocate, as his job as a collier allowed the couple some welcome income with which to build their life together in Hull, but Hannah and her son, Willie (Peace's beloved step-son), after deep consideration, replied that they would be joining Peace in London.

The eating house was quickly sold, and the proceeds brought to Peace on their arrival in order to fund a new living arrangement for this unusual extended family.

After firstly renting two adjoining houses in Billingsgate Street, Greenwich, Peace was curtly informed by Susan that she did not care for the area, and if she was expected to live in close proximity to her rival in Peace's affections, that this should be in an area which suited her, and was more appropriate to a couple of their comfortable means.

In May, 1877, Susan was granted her wish, although the relocation to the more affluent district of Peckham meant that the group would only be able to occupy one house. However, with Hannah and Willie occupying the basement, and Peace and Susan living separately on the other floors, the living arrangements at 5 East Terrace, Evelina Road, seemed to suit all the occupants.

Obtaining such a prestigious abode had been far from simple. Despite gathering all his loved ones under one roof, Peace's foremost thought had been for Tommy, his beloved pony. But, after some negotiation with the letting agent, it was decided that Peace could build a stable on the premises.

The agent, despite Peace's apparent wealth, had been wary of letting the premises to such an eccentric individual with an irregular entourage, and had asked for formal references before the contract could be signed. In response to this, Peace asked the agent to dine with him one evening, and with his innate ability to charm and spin yarns, Peace had soon persuaded the man that no references would be required.

The new house was very much the smart London townhouse, with steps leading to the front door, and down to the separate basement door. Behind the building was a generously sized garden, in which Tommy was allowed to wander to his heart's content and which stretched out until it reached a railway line. No doubt watching the trains pass by the end of his garden brought back memories for Peace, but despite this, the house was soon to be made homely in a style which could only be attributed to the lifestyle of its leaseholder.

Those who had visited 5 East Terrace described the interior to be as eccentric as its occupant, with oriental rugs, venetian blinds and grand gilded picture frames and mirrors taking up every inch that wasn't already occupied by a vast array of musical instruments, in all of which Peace seemed to be proficient.

The house was also a haven for animals of all kinds, with cages of exotic birds, rabbit hutches, and a plethora of cats and dogs enjoying the cosy interior of this outwardly prim and proper residence. For a man who had spent so much of his life behind bars or escaping the authorities, that was a paradise which could be stamped with his own personality.

Not only had the Thompsons settled into their new home, they were quickly becoming a very popular couple in Peckham society. Their new neighbours were fascinated by the odd couple who had moved into their street, especially the funny little man who sported a year-round tan and a multitude of different coloured wigs.

Peace often invited his neighbours to the house for evening gatherings, during which he would entertain his guests by playing a wide variety of musical instruments and engaging them in deep conversation. The usual topics would be the arts, the plight of the poor and the risky subject of politics.

At this time, the Russo-Turkish war was tearing apart the far reaches of the continent and Peace, as ever outspoken, often made clear his anger towards the British government for funding the 'cruel Turks', and bemoaning the futility of war in these enlightened times. Peace truly was becoming a product of his middle-class surroundings, yet made no secret that he hailed from working-class roots in a poor and scarcely represented area of the country.

Despite the exuberance of the host, these gatherings were always halted at around 10pm, with Susan explaining that her husband was in ill-health and could not tolerate being late to bed. At this point, guests would be ushered from the front door, no doubt with Peace quietly making his way out of the back door armed with an empty sack, a bag full of tools and his trusty revolver.

Such was the reputation of the mysterious Mr Thompson as a fine musician that it was a regular occurrence to see him walking through the dark streets carrying a violin case. Any onlooker would assume that he had been entertaining at a respectable gathering; yet, had anyone had cause to inspect the contents of the case, they would not find any instrument for making music, but an array of instruments crucial to breaking into a house.

Peace also became a regular at the local church and one of the most popular parishioners to attend Sunday services. Ironically, during Peace's renewal of faith, a burglar had broken into the church and attempted to steal several precious items. No doubt Peace breathed a huge sigh of relief as a description was circulated, describing a man in no way similar to himself. This was one crime which Peace did not commit; he had come too far to risk it all for a brass collection plate and a few candlesticks.

The mysterious Mr Thompson had greater things on his mind than petty theft. He was living in a city known as the workshop of the world, and as such, began to put his creative talents to legitimate use. He had made the acquaintance of a Mr Henry Fersey Brion, who described himself as an *inventor*. However, it would appear that Brion was not the success he portrayed to those who met him, as he was yet to invent anything of real value.

However, upon meeting the wily and perceptive man who had invited himself along to his workshop and covered his desk with a huge collection of drawings and notes, Brion knew he had found a kindred spirit, one who had ideas enough for the both of them, and also bore the skills required to bring these contraptions to life.

Whilst working together, the two men filed patents for such inventions as a smoke helmet to be used by firemen, an extendable brush for washing railway carriages, and most impressively, a contraption designed to raise sunken ships by displacing the water with gas, therefore allowing the vessel to rise slowly to the surface without the need of a crane.

With everything seemingly coming together in the remarkable life of Charlie Peace, it would seem that the hardship and misfortune which had previously followed him around the country like an unshakeable fierce dog had come to an end. However, it would only be a matter of time before unwonted drama would return to the Peace household.

As the year ended, and 1878 arrived, the idyllic lifestyle of the Thompsons began to fray at the seams. The first tragedy to hit was the death of Peace's pony, Tommy, who succumbed to a short illness with Peace, as ever, by his side and attending to his every need. The pony had been bought with the proceeds of Peace's first burglary in London: would this be a portent that they had outstayed their welcome?

The relationship between Peace and Susan Gray had also begun to fall apart at the seams, largely due to Susan's fondness for drink. On many occasions she had wandered from the house, and begun chatting to strangers in the street whilst under the influence of alcohol. Not only did Peace find this to be a distasteful reflection on the reputation he had worked so hard to build, but he was also wary of the secrets which could slip out during his partner's drunken ramblings.

Only too aware that it was Peace's talent for crime which provided food and lodgings for all involved, it was Hannah Peace who was charged with the responsibility of ensuring that Susan did not leave the house while inebriated. If she did, she quickly returned to face a venomous tongue-lashing from Mrs Peace, and, on several occasions, a brutal thrashing from Peace himself.

Not only was his home life suffering, but once again, Peace had been the victim of his own success. An astounding number of audacious burglaries had been reported over the last few months in South London, with hundreds of pounds worth of possessions being taken. In light of this, a special police unit was dispatched to the area, tasked with finding the burglar and bringing him to justice.

Ironically, one of the first to 'benefit' from these extra patrols was Peace himself, who found a policeman knocking on his door at the dead of night, having been alerted by a small light burning in the front room of the house. Peace explained that he had stayed up late to work on one of his inventions, and the policeman went cheerfully on his way. However, it is more likely that Peace had just returned from one of his regular moonlit expeditions.

Shortly after this came another of the moments of strange fortune with which Peace seems to have been blessed throughout his career. Whilst walking along Farringdon Road one evening, a Sheffield policeman who was visiting relatives in London almost bumped straight into the oncoming Peace, who, on this occasion, was bareheaded and dressed more casually than usual having been in a workshop putting the final touches to an invention.

The astute young policeman immediately recognised the man whom all of the South Yorkshire police force was hell-bent on bringing to justice. Seeing the flicker of recognition in the off-duty policeman's eyes, and instantly recognising a strong Yorkshire accent as he was addressed, Peace turned on his heels, and sprinted as quickly as his limp would allow him up the steps of Holborn Viaduct.

The policeman managed to catch up with his prey as they reached the top of the steps and Peace was within inches of having his collar felt, before twisting away in a moment of youthful agility and leaving the unfortunate constable clutching at thin air in the darkness of the viaduct.

Luckily for Peace, although the police had been alerted to a sighting in London of this most wanted man, the brilliance of his disguise, and his chameleon-like transformation into the alias of Mr Thompson left the London police with no clue that the friendly old man who loved animals and music was none other than Charles Peace, the Banner Cross Murderer.

Another lucky escape was to come soon after, as Peace continued his spree of South London burglaries in the face of an increased police presence, looking over his shoulder every moment for signs of danger. However, this time, the danger did not come from an outside threat; it came from his own complacency, and a rare lack of concentration.

Having climbed onto the portico of a wealthy house in Streatham, Peace made an uncharacteristic, yet potentially life-threatening misjudgement, losing his footing, and plummeting downwards onto a set of iron railings. Luckily for Peace, although painfully impaled through the shoulder, he managed to free himself and make his escape, no doubt heading for the nearest doctor with a hastily fabricated story.

With his latest injury requiring time to heal, the lack of income into the household was beginning to become a serious issue. Cajoled by Susan Gray, who found herself in an unwonted state of sobriety, and keen to regain his losses, Peace had no choice but to pack his violin case, say farewell to his lover, and once again head out into the night.

A handful of successful, yet low-key burglaries later, Peace was once again feeling invincible as he took the decision to step up to the serious business of burgling wealthy homes. Not only did the household need the money, but his pride needed the satisfaction of regaining his crown as the mystery cat-burglar of South London.

Having selected his target, a house in St John's Park, Blackheath, Peace set out just after midnight on 10 October 1878. He would reach his destination on foot, never having replaced his beloved Tommy, and by 2am he had reached his destination, having walked a slow and circuitous route in order not to arouse the suspicions of the policemen who seemed to have trebled in number over the last six months.

Shortly after 2am, Peace crept through the upstairs room of the house which belonged to a Mr Burness. An experienced policeman, Constable Robinson, was making his rounds of the area and was alerted to a light appearing suddenly in one of the back bedroom windows. Was this the work of the infamous Blackheath Burglar?

Quickly summoning two nearby colleagues, Robinson instructed one of the junior constables to approach the front door, while the other would take position in the alleyway along the side of the house. Robinson himself, his eyes still transfixed on the rear bedroom widow, would remain in the garden, and keep looking for the tiniest sign of movement.

As on the occasion at Peace's own home, the policeman who had approached the front of the house rang the doorbell in order to ascertain whether the residents were present. In light of the recent spree of burglaries, it was more favourable to wake a family from their slumber than to allow an habitual criminal to remain at large.

The sound of the doorbell echoed through the (almost) empty house and before the ringing had stopped, the waiting Constable Robinson was aghast to see a silhouetted figure leaping through the open dining room window before hurriedly making its way along the path towards the neighbouring street which ran to the rear of the house.

In the darkness of the garden, the figure had failed to spot the policeman lying in wait just yards away, but was alerted to this unwelcome presence as he heard the footsteps rapidly approaching behind him. As would be expected of any policemen in the line of duty, Robinson had immediately given chase to the quickly retreating shadow.

The burglar turned on hearing the footsteps, bellowing 'Keep back, or by God I'll shoot you!' whilst reaching into his deep coat pocket for his revolver. However, with the same level of bravado exhibited by Arthur Dyson just a couple of years before, and in repeat of the tenacity of the poor young Constable Cock, killed in Whalley Range, Constable Robinson maintained his pursuit.

Three shots quickly rang out in the Blackheath night, each of them passing close to the oncoming policeman. Growing ever nearer to his prey, Robinson then heard the report of another shot which whistled by his head. At this point, the younger man was almost upon the burglar and leapt at his foe, delivering a hefty blow to the man's face.

Entangled in a knot of limbs and desperately making every attempt to free himself, the would-be assassin managed to loosen the policeman's grip on his right hand. Shouting 'I'll settle you this time!' he managed to angle the revolver towards his captor, and pulled the trigger.

The bullet passed through Constable Robinson's upper arm from point blank range, yet, despite the excruciating pain, the policeman did not loosen his grip on the prisoner. Although seriously injured, the dutiful constable was able to overpower his older attacker, and flung him to the ground with considerable force.

Taking hold of the revolver which had, just seconds earlier, been pointed directly at him, Constable Robinson used the weapon to deliver a heavy blow to the top the assailant's head, rendering him unconscious. The famously elusive Charles Frederick Peace had finally been captured - done for by his own trusty revolver.

Chapter 10

The First Judgement

'Why has government been instituted at all? Because the
passions of man will not conform to the dictates of reason
and justice without constraint.'
Alexander Hamilton, Politician, Economist and
Political Philosopher, 1755-1804

T he prisoner was unceremoniously slung into a vacant cell at
Greenwich Police Station; limp, bleeding, and muttering
incoherently. Despite his injuries and current condition, this was
as good as life was going to get for him. Dazed and bewildered he
sprawled on the cold floor, temporarily, yet blissfully, unaware of the
grave predicament in which he would soon find himself.

Upon awaking, the wretched Burglar of Blackheath wasted no time
devoting his energy to all manner of complaints and gripes. In the mind of
the prisoner, he was cold, he was gravely injured, and he was being falsely
imprisoned. Yet, as the profanities echoed around the police station, his
captors still had no idea whom they had bundled into the cell just hours before.

This kind of tirade came naturally to Charlie Peace; he was not a man
who was used to being on the receiving end of a physical blow and
certainly not the kind of character who would raise his hands in surrender.
No doubt as furious with himself as he was with those who kept him
prisoner, Peace would certainly not be co-operating with any enquires.

His first course of action was to remain silent. Having been asked
several times to identify himself, Peace had refused to answer. The crimes
for which he was currently being remanded in custody were serious, but
not as serious as the crimes for which he had yet to receive justice. A story
had to be concocted, and a lengthy silent protest was the option available
to Peace as he strove to buy himself every possible second in which to
think his way out of trouble.

CHARLIE PEACE

Although still dressed in the modest clothing in which he performed his nocturnal trade, Peace was still far from recognisable as the Banner Cross Murderer. His frequent and liberal use of walnut oil had altered his colouring semi-permanently, to the point that the police recorded the details of their prisoner as 'a half-caste, about sixty years of age.'

For a Caucasian man in his forties, this was quite the endorsement of the talents he held for disguise. However, less pleasing to Peace would have been the comment written alongside the official description, which described the prisoner as having a 'repellent aspect', although, with his gnarled features and ability to dislocate his bottom jaw, it is hardly surprising that the police were instantly struck by the unique ugliness of their prisoner.

Indeed, it was by this very description that Peace was listed in the records of the magistrate before whom he appeared the following morning. Again, the elderly and volatile man who stood silently in the dock refused to utter even a single word during the proceedings, speaking only to berate the policemen who roughly manhandled him back to his cell.

The inability to correctly identify the defendant left the magistrate with only one option - to detain the prisoner until such time as he was willing to co-operate. Peace was initially remanded for seven days and transferred to the notorious Newgate Gaol, pending another appearance in the dock. He knew that he could remain silent no longer; he had a family and a mistress to take into account, and therefore would have to make contact with the outside world.

Making contact with those who could provide a link between his current anonymity and the previous crimes which he was desperately trying to conceal, would be far too risky. Peace needed a middle man, someone who would come to his aid, but knew nothing of his nefarious past. However, persuading an acquaintance to visit him in his cell, without giving away either his past identity as Charlie Peace or his more reputable persona of Mr Thompson, would be difficult.

In a moment of inspiration Peace settled upon a plan where he would send a letter, intriguing enough in its content, to persuade his contact to visit if only to solve the mystery of the strange man who had so pitifully requested his assistance from behind the high walls of Newgate.

The recipient was none other than Henry Brion, the inventor with whom Peace had filed several patents. Knowing his former colleague to be of an inquisitive nature and with a good heart, Peace began to pen a letter, taking care not to reveal anything of himself or his family in its contrived contents. The letter, which was soon followed by others, proved to be of sufficient intrigue as to reel in his former friend.

In one of the letters, which was later used in evidence, it is apparent that Peace had deliberately feigned a show of illiteracy. Portraying himself as a thoroughly repentant man who had lost his way owing to drink, Peace ends the letter by stating that a visit from Mr Brion would 'hease his trobel hart' and asking him not to despise him 'as his own famery has don.' Peace signed the letter as 'John Ward', and awaited the outcome.

The plan had paid off, and just a few days later a confused and befuddled Mr Brion arrived at Newgate asking to be granted an audience with the mysterious 'John Ward'. As expected by Peace, the prison warders were expecting this as they had carefully read the letter several times before delivering it to the intended recipient.

However, as successful as the ruse had been, the outcome of the unusual visit was to prove fruitless. Mr Brion was aghast to see his former colleague in such a situation and agreed to keep the identity of Mr Ward (who was known to Brion as Mr Thompson) to himself for the foreseeable future, but was unable to provide any information as to the current wellbeing of his family or of Susan.

With his latest persona now brought to life, Peace was able to re-use the moniker he had created in order to write another letter. This time the recipient would be closer to home. Knowing that this would inevitably lead to the discovery of his residence in Peckham and his alias as Mr Thompson, Peace had made a deal with the devil; he would risk standing trial as John Thompson if need be, but could not risk the sentence which would be handed down to Charles Peace.

The letter was quickly written and sent for the attention of 'Mrs Ward' who, coincidentally, shared the same address as Susan Gray. The contents were, again, a work of art with the penitent John Ward bemoaning his drunken misadventure and claiming that he had 'never been in prison before.' However, as ingenious as the contents of the letter may have been, they were to be delivered to an empty house.

Upon Peace's failure to return home on that eventful night, panic had ensued in the extended household. However unreliable a father and husband, the head of the household had never failed to return in a timely fashion from one of his nocturnal trips. Something was amiss, and by first light the following morning, the house was on full alert.

Within hours the more dubious contents of 5 East Terrace had been packed into boxes and loaded onto a hastily arranged cart. In the midst of the frantic packing, Willie, Peace's stepson, had been tasked to take a walk and keep his ear to the ground with regard to any news of their missing patriarch. It was not long before he hurried home with unwanted news.

The events of the previous evening were the talk of the town. The attempted murder of a policeman who had interrupted the infamous Blackheath Burglar was front page news, as was the subsequent capture and arrest of the man who had, up until now, succeeded in relieving many of the wealthier South London residents of their prized possessions.

By the time Peace had been transferred to Newgate as an anonymous prisoner, his family and possessions had also been transferred, back to Nottingham, and to the house of Susan's sister, where the shell-shocked group stayed in fear of reprisal by the London police.

Two days later, and with Peace still languishing in prison, Hannah Peace decided to return to her native Sheffield, and with the devoted Willie in tow, made an unexpected arrival at the home of her daughter, a house in Hazel Street, in which the newly married Jane lived with her husband, who must have been wondering what kind of family he had married into.

Peace's entourage was safe, for now, but hundreds of miles away, the man himself was anything but safe. The police were doggedly trying to piece together the true identity of John Ward, and had already visited 5 East Terrace, having made the connection between the mysterious Mr Ward, and the popular and eccentric John Thompson.

The link between the two had actually been provided by Mr Brion, who had wasted no time in requesting a meeting with the governor of Newgate in order to alleviate himself of any guilt in relation to the deception in which he found himself embroiled. This would not be the last time Mr Brion would betray the confidence of his former colleague.

Having satisfied themselves that nothing of any interest had been left behind by the family in Peckham, the police began to dig around the neighbourhood for any information as to the whereabouts of the previous residents. Very little was known of the occupants of the unusual household, and the little that was known, proved to be a web of lies and deception.

However, it was mentioned to the police by local acquaintances that the woman masquerading as Mrs Thompson was originally from Nottingham, something perhaps mentioned during one of Susan's frequent drunken walks around the neighbourhood. This was the best hope of any kind of promising lead, so a group of London's finest were packed off to the Midlands, in search of the missing Susan Thompson.

It would appear that Peace's desperate escape from the Nottingham police during his time living in the Marsh had come back to haunt him, as when their London counterparts arrived and began to ask questions, the description of the couple matched very closely that of the burglar and his wife who had been so lucky to escape the city without capture.

Susan Thompson was none other than Susan Gray, who was now confusing matters by using her original married name of Susan Bailey. However, with a fondness for the darker side of life, and a drinking habit which was almost legendary in the Marsh, it would be no surprise to learn that Peace's lover was known to the Nottingham police, having been accommodated overnight on many occasions due to her inebriated state.

It would appear that the police located Susan very quickly, yet no arrest was made, and no items were confiscated from the home of her sister. However, almost instantly upon leaving the presence of Mrs Bailey, the police were once again on the move, travelling further north, this time to Sheffield. Perhaps Susan wasn't such a devoted mistress after all?

Brooding silently in his cell, Peace was still unaware of the events which had taken place since his arrest, and had no idea that the wheels of justice were in motion, with every turn leading the police closer to identifying the man who referred to himself as John Ward. Had he known that the police were about to arrive in South Yorkshire he would have known that the end of his act was near.

It was 6 November 1878 when the door of Mr Bolsover's house in Hazel Road seemed to explode under the force of several policemen.

Finding the unfortunate owner to be away at work, the intrepid investigators did, however, find that the house was occupied. Cowering at the kitchen table and shaking with fear were the elusive Hannah Peace and her long-suffering daughter.

The two shaken women were detained until the house had been thoroughly searched from top to bottom, and as it transpired, only one of the women was to be released on the completion of the investigation. The boxes which had been removed from Peckham, via Nottingham, to Sheffield had been easily located, and their contents proved to be more damaging than Mrs Peace could have imagined.

Aside from the valuable contents of the boxes, all of which had been reported missing in previous months, there were items of far less monetary value which had been included during the frantic packing. However, to the police who had travelled so far to uncover the identity of their prisoner, these items were worth their weight in gold.

The jewellery, silverware, paintings and other objets d'art had been of use; so much so that Hannah Peace now found herself in the humiliating position of being returned to London to face charges of receiving stolen goods. But it was a small bundle of papers which bore the real value in this treasure trove - a bundle of papers which would betray their currently incarcerated owner.

Ordinarily, the bundle of creased papers which nestled between the other gold and silver items in the box would have been largely ignored. However, as the main reason for this cross-country investigation was to identify the man who had silently stared into the distance when appearing in the dock, these papers were of great interest to many people.

One can only surmise that these items were never meant to be discovered, yet here they were. Letters, pawn shop receipts, and other personal effects, all of which did not belong to the fictional Mr Thompson. The name that appeared on many of the documents was anything but fictional; it was the name of a man who was certainly real, a fact which could be testified to by a grieving wife, and a multitude of burglary victims.

The name on the creased papers was 'Charles Peace', the very name which the assembled policemen had hoped to uncover since their brief visit to Nottingham. Undoubtedly, this discovery was far beyond the hopes of all involved; a team of dedicated men who had been sent to find the identity of a burglar had, in fact, uncovered the identity of England's most wanted murderer.

This was strong circumstantial evidence, but could still be challenged in any reasonably fair court of law. The police needed a positive visual identification from someone who knew Charlie Peace, and as the men began their journey back to London, they had with them two extra travellers - an unnamed Sheffield constable who had known Peace during his time in Darnall, and an unnamed woman, who swore that she had looked into the eyes of a killer.

Upon arrival in London, the two witnesses were transported directly to Newgate Gaol, where they would be put to the test. Joining the governor in the exercise yard, the constable watched as the remand prisoners walked solemnly in the cold morning air. There were five prisoners in the yard that morning, and it took the constable just a matter of seconds to identify the man whose crimes had brought him hundreds of miles from home.

Looking away as the small, strange-looking man limped past, the Sheffield police constable paused until he was safely out of earshot. With one more definitive look, he then turned inconspicuously to the warder and said quietly 'That's Peace, I'd know him anywhere.'

The sight of a policeman in the exercise yard was not unusual in the remand wing of Newgate, but something seemed to bother the limping man who, after pausing for thought, hobbled towards the constable and quietly asked: 'What do you want me for?' before being told in no uncertain terms by the warder to continue his chilly morning exercise.

Although the sight of a policeman in the exercise yard was not unusual, the sight of a middle-aged woman would certainly have drawn unwonted attention. The other extra passenger to have been brought to London watched intently from a distance before turning to the police officer who had accompanied her and, like the Sheffield constable just moments before, confirming that the man shuffling through the winter fog was none other than Charlie Peace.

Peace was only to officially learn that his secrets had been uncovered during his plea hearing at the Old Bailey. However, although Peace was willing to plead guilty for his crimes in Blackheath, he seemed unmoved by the revelation and maintained the pretence that he had never heard of anyone named Charles Peace.

Despite the eventual identification of the prisoner, when Peace finally appeared on trial at the Old Bailey on 19 November 1878 for burglary and attempted murder, he did so under the name of John Ward *alias* Charles Peace. Strangely, his age was also given incorrectly as Peace was listed as being sixty years old rather than his true age of forty seven.

These oversights, usually meticulously checked in any court of law, let alone the Old Bailey, perhaps suggest that, given the previous unpunished crimes of the man who now stood in the dock, the trial which he was about to stand was something of a technicality, a formality which must be completed before a much more serious judgement could take place.

Formality or not, the trial had necessitated the services of one of Britain's foremost high court judges, Sir Henry Hawkins, a man who was well known for taking no nonsense from the wretched souls who appeared before him in the dock. This was itself a serious matter, without even taking into account Peace's earlier crimes.

The evidence against Peace was overwhelming; he had been caught in the act of burglary, and had fired a revolver at the very policeman who had been alerted to the break-in. However, the main problem for Peace was that, unlike his previous crimes, this time there was a living witness to identify him.

Peace sat passively throughout the proceedings; he was well aware that there were no loopholes to be found, no holes in the evidence to be discovered. This ordinarily volatile little man spoke only to confirm his inaccurate name and date of birth, and it wasn't until his defence counsel was given the chance to speak that Peace finally began to stir in the dock.

Mr Montagu Williams, who had been tasked with defending the indefensible, had also remained silent for the majority of the proceedings, knowing that he had only one avenue of hope in this whole matter; the outcome of the trial rested on whether Mr Justice Hawkins believed that Peace had intended to kill Constable Robinson.

Calling Peace to give evidence, Williams began his defence with the flimsy notion that the revolver with which Constable Robinson was shot 'went off easily'; a notion which was further maintained by Peace, as he was given the chance to plead with Mr Justice Hawkins for mercy. Standing shakily before the judge, the eccentric prisoner pleaded:

> 'I really did not know that the pistol was loaded, and I hope, my lord, that you will have mercy on me. I feel that I have disgraced myself; I am not fit either to live or die. I am not prepared to meet my God, but still I feel that my career has been made to appear much worse than it really is.
>
> Oh, my lord, do have mercy on me; do give me one chance of repenting and of preparing to meet my God. Do, my lord, have mercy on me; and I assure you that you shall never repent it. As you hope for mercy yourself at the hands of the great God, do have mercy on me, and give me a chance of redeeming my character and preparing myself to meet my God. I pray, and beseech you to have mercy upon me.'

However, this impassioned plea from a seemingly elderly prisoner fell upon deaf ears. Mr Justice Hawkins had presided over more than his fair share of trials, and was no stranger to a prisoner affecting an air of senility or madness in order to receive a less severe punishment. Peace would have to bear the consequences of his own actions.

Before passing sentence, the judge took the opportunity to admonish Mr Williams for his laughable attempt at portraying the shooting as an accident, reminding him that the gun must have 'gone off accidentally' five times during Peace's escape attempt and that, had Constable Robinson not held his arm in front of his face, Peace would have been standing trial for (another) murder.

Upon passing sentence, Mr Justice Hawkins took great care to avoid any mention of the crimes for which Peace had yet to stand trial and also stated that there were no merits to be gained in examining Peace's criminal career as a whole, the matters for which he was now being sentenced were serious enough on their own to merit a severe sentence.

Sentencing Peace to penal servitude for life, the judge commented that for a man of sixty, Peace was lucky to have only received this sentence in his advancing years, as he had no doubt been lucky to avoid such a sentence in his younger years. With the cruel irony of this comment still ringing in his ears, the forty-seven-year-old Peace was led from the dock.

No longer on remand, and with an uncertain future to look forward to, Peace was transported to the squalid and notoriously harsh Pentonville prison, where he would begin his life sentence. However, given how his life had finally turned out, penal servitude for life was the very best that Peace could now hope for.

As for Hannah Peace, she was also to stand trial at the Old Bailey for receiving stolen goods; however, as her common-law husband had already been jailed for life and proved to be a violent man with a tempestuous temper, she was quickly acquitted on the grounds of having acted under the influence of her domineering husband.

Returning to Sheffield, Hannah no doubt breathed a sigh of relief at her acquittal, but equally feared a future without the income provided by the nocturnal escapades of her husband. She rejoined her daughter and son-in-law and began a new life, a life without luxury or extravagance but also a life without violence or crime.

Meanwhile, in Nottingham, a woman was drafting a letter to the Treasury laying claim to a £100 reward for information leading to the capture of Charles Frederick Peace, the Banner Cross Murderer. The claim was based on information which had been supplied to the police on 5 November 1878, the day before Mr Bolsover's door was so rudely kicked in.

Just days later, a polite reply was received, in which Mrs S. Bailey *alias* Thompson was advised to go through the correct channels, and take her request to the Home Office.

Chapter 11

The 05:15 to Sheffield

*'It is vain for the coward to flee; death follows close behind,
it is only by defying it that the brave escape.'*
Voltaire , Author, 1694-1778

Peace had been brooding overnight, pacing the small cell in Pentonville prison which had been his home for the last month. The cause of his obvious unease was a surprise trip taken the day before, a rare trip beyond the high walls of his current residence. But there had been no joy upon reaching his destination, what followed had been a day of humiliation and torment.

He had been awakened early on the bitterly cold morning of 16 January 1879, and told to dress. Just minutes later, he was joined in his cell by two warders, who led him through the dilapidated prison until they reached the outer gates, where he was bundled into a waiting carriage and transported through the streets of London. The destination was Kings Cross station where he was chained and bound before being led to a nearby platform.

His frequent trips around the country during his days of freedom, and his knowledge of the railway routes, meant that Peace was in no doubt as to where he was being taken. He had answered for his crimes in London, but there was a small matter which had yet to be resolved, a matter of murder in his hometown.

Having been positively identified as Charles Peace, the escaped murderer of Banner Cross, before his trial at the Old Bailey, he would have known that this cross country trip was inevitable. His life had been reduced to a meagre existence behind bars, but at least he still *had* a life. This trip, however, was to decide for how much longer he would be granted his very existence.

He had always known that Arthur Dyson was dead, killed by a bullet

115

from his very own revolver. He had even seen the reward posters bearing his name and description. However, his talent for disguise and criminal cunning had led him to believe that being captured was but a small concern during his new life in London.

The penalty for wilful murder was death, and that was exactly what he would be charged with when he reached his final destination that day. He was being taken home to Sheffield to answer a charge of murder, and he knew that feelings in his hometown would be running high on his return. He had to find a way out; the lion-hearted Charles Peace had been reduced to a coward, terrified of being sentenced to meet his maker.

Upon boarding the train, Peace was seated on a bench at the far end of a carriage between his two guards. This was to be a long and tiring journey, and the only hope he had of escaping the clutches of the Sheffield magistrates was to find a way to escape.

He had to find a way to become free from his chains, and decided that the best chance of freedom would come in a moment where he could escape the clutches of his guards for just one brief moment. Asking to use the toilet, the chains which secured him to the wrists of the two warders were removed, to be replaced by a pair of handcuffs and ankle chains, which allowed him sufficient movement to attend to his ablutions.

However, the two warders were no fools, and made sure that they had checked the toilet for any possible escape routes before allowing Peace to relieve himself in privacy. They also took the precaution of standing directly outside the tiny convenience, listening for any signs of suspicious activity.

Not even the unique mind of Charlie Peace could conjure up a method of escape from this travelling fortress, but he would not be defied so easily. Several times he requested to visit the convenience, until the warders had had enough. They bluntly informed him that he would not be released from his chains again until they reached their destination.

As it turned out, his arrival in Sheffield was every bit as unpleasant as he had imagined. The party was greeted by a large crowd upon reaching the train station from which he had travelled so many times in the past. Order was only kept owing to a large number of police keeping the crowds at bay until the carriage which carried the three travellers into the town centre had disappeared into the distance.

The formalities of the day, however, turned out to be much less strenuous than the journey. Arriving at the imposing Town Hall, Peace was quickly bundled through a side entrance, and whisked into a waiting courtroom. This was exactly what he had expected, but the sight of the crowd which had attended the proceedings in order to catch a glimpse of this infamous killer immediately put paid to any sense of bravado he may have been harbouring.

Expecting to be immediately put on trial for his actions some years previously, Peace was no doubt relieved to find that he was attending his own preliminary hearing. However, the sight of one particular witness would have set alarm bells ringing as to his chances of escaping the trial with his life. There, in the crowded courtroom sat Kate Dyson, the widow of his victim.

But despite her attendance in court, no testimony was required on this occasion. This was a day for tedious formality and seemingly endless bureaucracy. By the time the court had seen fit to even acknowledge the prisoner, all that was required was for Peace to confirm his name, and that he understood the charges being brought against him, both of which he answered with a cursory, monosyllabic response.

No sooner had he performed the required duties than Peace was once again bundled back into a carriage to be taken to the train station and from there the whole tiresome journey was repeated in reverse, until, once again, he found himself, bewildered and enraged, pacing the floor of his cell in Pentonville.

And now, on the very next morning, he was to make the same journey again. But this time Peace had no intention of arriving at his destination. One way or another, he would not be arriving in Sheffield to another angry mob, and another day closer to the ultimate punishment. There had to be a way to escape.

The arrangements of the previous day had been repeated to the tiniest detail, the same warders, the same carriage, and, unfortunately for Peace, the very same train, on which he had found no possible means of escape. But he was not to be deterred; he had no intention of giving his hometown crowds the show they so desperately yearned for.

Chained once again to the two guards, he decided to try his luck, and hopefully requested to be allowed to use the toilet. However, on this occasion, one thing *had* changed. With a wry smile, one of the warders reached into his pocket and pulled out a small bag made of waxed paper. There would be no moments of solitude, or precious minutes to concoct an escape plan today; the bags had been supplied with the sole purpose of being used by Peace to relieve himself into.

With a distinct lack of privacy, the prisoner turned himself and faced the corner of the carriage, using the bag, which he then held out to the nearest warder. With a look of disgust, the warder nodded towards his colleague, who lowered the window and told Peace to throw the bag onto the tracks.

This disregard for the privacy and comfort of the prisoner had actually provided Peace with an opportunity, but with all his eggs currently being in the same basket, this closely-watched criminal genius could not let on that this was to his advantage, and instead spent the next hour complaining of his treatment at the hands of the crass and uncaring guards.

With apparent resignation to his fate, Peace spent the next hour or two gazing through the window. It would have appeared to his keepers that this was a condemned man, taking in the beauty of the English countryside for one last time before being closed away in a confined cell until the day he would meet his fate at the hands of the executioner.

But Peace was feeling anything but sentimental; he watched the fields and small settlements roll by until the landscape became more familiar. As the train was leaving the Midlands and crossing the boundary into South Yorkshire, Peace, once again asked for a bag into which to relieve himself. This was duly handed over to him, and his chains were again unfastened.

With one eye on attending to his business, and the other still transfixed on the view from the window, he turned to face the corner of the carriage, as was his cursory nod towards Victorian decency. Completing his task, he once again held out the bag, to be nodded with disdain in the direction of the window as before.

Being manacled, Peace was unable to reach the top of the window to dispose of the bag and its unpleasant contents, so the sliding frame was pulled down far enough for him to drop the bag from the moving train. This was the first mistake the two warders had made in the last two days, and one which they would live to regret.

Charlie Peace only needed one chance, and it only needed to be the slimmest of half-chances. This was a man who could scale a wall in seconds, and squeeze through the tiniest window without a sound. His pronounced limp and premature aging would often lull his prey into a false sense of security, until the moment came when he would spring into action in the blink of an eye.

This was the blink of the eye, the drop of the hat, and the heartbeat in which Peace would strike. However, on this occasion, the goal wasn't wealth or revenge, it was freedom. He wasn't a man who would go to his death without a fight; they would have to drag him kicking, screaming, biting and cursing into the dock.

As the wind swept through the open window, the time had come. Peace took a flying leap through the window, a manoeuvre requiring a great deal of agility, certainly more agility than the two guards had credited their prisoner with.

Expecting to hit the ground with bone-shattering force as the train sped past Kiveton Park, near Worksop, on the borders of Nottinghamshire and Yorkshire, Peace found himself to be hanging by the foot. It would appear that Peace had also made a misjudgement; he had misjudged the speed and reactions of his guards.

One of the warders had made a grab for his quickly disappearing foot as he theatrically attempted to take his leave of the train, and despite the twisting and thrashing of his prized catch, he was holding onto it for dear life. No amount of struggling seemed to loosen the hold of the warder's impressive grip.

The window, despite being tall enough to accommodate the flying frame of Peace, wasn't very wide. This meant that the other guard was useless to assist, as the shoulders of his colleague were blocking the frame. Instead, he frantically pulled at the communication cord, only to find that it wasn't in working order and hadn't been tested before the journey began, something which could be attributed as a second error on the part of Peace's keepers.

As his colleague sprinted along the corridor to find assistance, the guard with the vice-like grip was beginning to tire. Peace had, by this time, managed to catch hold of a footplate, and was pulling himself away from his captor with all his might, while furiously attempting to kick out with his free foot.

Eventually, the forces of gravity and resistance came to the aid of the prisoner, and he managed to work himself free, leaving the guard with only an empty shoe in his stiff and aching hands. Peace had made his escape from his captors and from the train, but had hit the ground with a sickening thud for his troubles.

Further along the train, the other guard had found assistance in two businessmen, who had finally managed to find a section of communication cord that was operable. But by now, the train had covered almost two miles since their important cargo had slipped from the grasp of his keepers, and it would take another mile for the train to come to a halt.

By the time the train had slowed sufficiently for the two guards to begin their dash along the tracks towards their lost prisoner, Peace had not moved an inch; instead, he lay bleeding and unconscious on the footway, having crashed head-first onto the frozen ground at high speed. He was lucky, or perhaps unlucky, to be alive.

Peace would later inform his stepson, Willie Ward, that this had been no escape attempt; it had been a suicide attempt. Wishing to end his life on his own terms and in an area of the country he considered to be home. It is more likely that Peace was prepared for either eventuality, but would rather admit to a failed suicide attempt than a failed escape.

'I saw from the way I was guarded all the way down from London and back when I came for my first trial, that I could not get away from the warders, and I knew I could not jump from an express train without being killed.

I took a look at Darnall as I went down and went back, and after I was put in my cell, I thought it all over. I felt that I could not get away, and then I made my mind up to kill myself.

I got two pieces of paper and pricked on them the words "Bury me at Darnall, God bless you all" with a bit of black dirt that I found on the floor of my cell. I wrote the same on another piece of paper, and then I hid them in my clothes.

My hope was, as I jumped from the train, I would be cut to pieces under the wheels. Then I should have been taken to the Duke of York (a pub in Darnall) and there would have been an inquest over me. As soon as the inquest was over you would have claimed my body, found the pieces of paper, and then you would have buried me at Darnall.'

From this statement, it does appear that Peace was resigned to die as he hit the ground, but it is also difficult to imagine that, had he miraculously landed unharmed, he would not have fled across the fields towards freedom, leaving another chapter of folklore in his wake.

As it was, Peace had failed on both counts. He regained consciousness as the warders wrapped him in their coats, and knew that his luck had finally run out. A slow train, also heading to Sheffield, soon came to the aid of the group, and as soon as he was lifted into the guard's van, he once again closed his eyes and slipped back into unconsciousness.

The leap from the train had come at some physical cost for this aging villain. A profusely bleeding scalp wound and a multitude of cuts and bruises had been the only gain from this whole experience. But he was not the only disappointed person in Sheffield by the time he reached the relative comfort of a police cell.

The announcement in court that Peace would not be present on that day, and that the proceedings would be indefinitely postponed was met with sighs and groans of disappointment from the crowds who had gathered to catch a glimpse of Sheffield's most infamous son. The disappointed public and unneeded officials would have read with interest this article which appeared in the next morning's edition of the *Sheffield Star*.

'Peace's career continues to be one series of surprises, not the least astonishing of which has been discovered this morning. His object in jumping from the train yesterday morning appears to have been not so much to escape, but to destroy himself.

He has very often been heard to express a desire to be buried in Darnall, as many associations appear to have endeared the place to him... . It is also a remarkable fact that the spot selected by Peace at which to make his daring leap from the carriage was almost within sight of the spires of Darnall church.'

Those with any interest in Peace's wellbeing, be it for empathetic or purely selfish reasons, would have also read with interest another article printed on the same page of the same newspaper, which reported in detail the condition of the Banner Cross murderer since his spectacular leap from the speeding train:

'A very large proportion of the public will be glad to hear that Charles Peace has progressed satisfactorily through the night, and is much better this morning. It will, perhaps, almost be a matter of history to state what is the matter with him, and how he came to be in the condition he is in.

When being conveyed to Sheffield yesterday morning with two warders, he succeeded, when near to Kiveton Park station, in jumping through the window of the carriage, and was stunned by the fall and wounded in the head.

When first carried to the cell he occupies, it was apprehended that he had received a severe concussion to his brain, and was otherwise injured. There were others, knowing what an arch-deceiver he is, who believed that he was not half so bad as he made out to be.

One officer, who has had a good deal to do with him, remarked that a good ash stick would bring him round sooner than medicine.'

Peace had spent the night in a Sheffield police cell and refused to take any medication until the offer of a medicinal brandy was repeated once again later that night. Appearing to be suffering from concussion and exposure, due to sprawling unconscious on the frozen ground, he had refused to speak, instead spending his evening covered by a pile of rugs.

A surgeon, Dr Hallam, was called to assess his injuries and found that Peace's condition was not life-threatening in any way. So confident was he of this he refused to be called back again to the police station in regards to this particular prisoner. He would call in again at a reasonable hour in the morning to monitor any progress made overnight.

Indeed, when Dr Hallam did return the next morning he found a prisoner who claimed to be too injured and ill to emerge from beneath his pile of rugs, but who had also polished off several mugs of tea and the best part of a loaf of bread with butter, along with several more 'medicinal' brandies.

The two warders remained in possession of their dastardly ward, and despite their obvious error in allowing a prisoner to approach an open window, the Sheffield Star spoke of their dedication to their duties with glowing praise in the aftermath of such an eventful day.

'The two warders who brought him from London have never left him since they picked him up from the railway yesterday morning. One of them has sat close by Peace's side throughout the whole night, watching his every movement, and not for an instant having his gaze averted from his now more than ever remarkable and distinguished prisoner.

At intervals, Peace has, as stated, tossed around a good deal, and then he has become quiet and apparently dropped into a sound slumber. Presently, the watchful eye of the warder has seen him peep stealthily from beneath his rugs, evidently to ascertain whether he might risk any move without being watched. Of course, there was not the slightest chance of him escaping from the cells.'

And so the trial of Charles Peace had been postponed, but not avoided by any means. Despite his ambitious attempt at whatever choice he had made between freedom and suicide, this once menacing and violent criminal now lay physically and mentally broken beneath a pile of rugs in a police cell, just a stone's throw from the courtroom he had so viciously fought to avoid.

Chapter 12

The Second Judgement

'Peace is more important than all justice; and peace was not made
for the sake of justice, but justice for the sake of peace.'
Martin Luther, Religious Leader, 1483-1546

A loud exclamation of 'Let Charles Peace stand forward!' was the signal for the over-crowded courtroom to fall silent in anticipation of the most unwelcome homecoming the people of Sheffield had ever mustered. A quiet shuffle of feet was followed by a gasp from those in attendance as a frail-looking man, his head bound in bandages, meekly entered the dock.

A charge of wilful murder was read to the prematurely aged man, whose gaze did not lift from the floor of the dock. 'How say you, Charles Peace, are you guilty or not guilty?' came the question from the clerk of the court. 'Not guilty,' muttered the prisoner.

Broken, bandaged, and all but defeated, the ever-elusive Charles Frederick Peace had finally been successfully delivered to his hometown on 23 January 1879, where he was to face another powerful exhibition of justice for his crimes. This time the punishment was to be for the murder of Arthur Dyson, an act of violence which still burned in the hearts and minds of the people of Sheffield.

Peace would freely admit that the unfortunate Mr Dyson had died at his hand, but defiantly refused to accept the charge of wilful murder; this whole sorry state of affairs had been an accident, he had claimed. A struggle in the dark and a faulty revolver had been to blame claimed the defendant. But, in the eyes of those present, he was guilty and all that was left was for the punishment to be decided.

His deliverance into the hands of the Sheffield authorities had been carried out as quietly as possible. This time, the police could afford no mistakes and in the knowledge that a publically heralded arrival would bring a baying mob to greet their prisoner home, they had ensured that all parties had remained in the dark about this most controversial homecoming.

Peace himself had been surprised that he was, once again, woken early and bundled from his cell in Pentonville Prison and into a waiting cab along with three guards. With his wounds bandaged, and his concussion having been deemed by a prison doctor to be all but gone, it had been decided that he was fit to stand trial. The people of Sheffield were demanding justice, and the London authorities were only too happy to assist.

Having once again been conveyed northwards by train (although much closer attention was paid to the prisoner this time), there had been no crowd to greet this unusual party. The only stop was the West Bar Police Station (now the Police and Fire Museum) almost in the heart of the modern city centre, where Peace was held in a basement cell until the court was ready to receive him

Just before noon another waiting cab then hurriedly delivered Peace and his guards to the Town Hall (which doubled as a courtroom on such auspicious occasions), where Peace's involvement in the murder of Arthur Dyson was to be examined by a group of magistrates, Messrs Welby, Rodgers, Fisher, Roberts, Hallam and Laycock.

The morning had been spent discussing the case and the police used this period of closed court to give the assembled magistrates a blow by blow account of the Banner Cross shooting. By the time Peace arrived, it was straight to business. Time was beginning to tick away and word of Peace's ensuing appearance had spread. The court was beginning to heave at the seams with onlookers, desperate to catch a glimpse of this famous villain.

Due to his injuries and general ill health, Peace was allowed the small comfort of being seated in the dock, his bandaged head just peeking over the railings. The stipendiary magistrate, Mr Welby, who was to lead the proceedings, was keen to ensure that the hearing moved along as swiftly as possible, and invited the prosecution counsel to address the court.

Peace's solicitor, Mr W.H. Clegg, was something of a local celebrity already, having been a former footballer for both Sheffield Wednesday and England. However, his task on this day was an unenviable one, and his first motion was to ask the court for an adjournment, on the grounds that he had only been assigned to the case that morning, and had yet to meet Peace in person.

'I appear for the prisoner, and my application is that he be remanded, on various grounds. The principal ground on which I base my application is that I was only instructed this morning to appear on behalf of the prisoner. It has been impossible, therefore, for me to get full instructions in order to conduct the defence of my client.

The prisoner has only been brought from London this morning, and I could not have a personal interview with him before. Moreover, I understand that, until yesterday, the prisoner had no knowledge that the Treasury intended to bring him to Sheffield to be placed on trial.

The prosecution has had a great deal of time for the purpose of getting up the prosecution against the prisoner. They have had various interviews with the witnesses who they are going to call for the prosecution, and I think it would have only been fair to give the prisoner some idea of what was to be done with him, so he might have had ample opportunity to instruct his solicitor in his defence.'

However, this perfectly reasonable request was immediately refused by the magistrates, who saw no legal grounds to halt the proceedings, especially as the witnesses were present in the courtroom. Indeed they also believed the evidence to be so strongly in favour of the prosecution that no benefit would be gained by the defence in postponing the hearing. The counsel for the prosecution, Mr Pollard, agreed, stating:

'It would only be fair on my part to say that I have no wish whatever to hurry the proceedings unnecessarily. But this is not the first time my friend, Mr Clegg, has had an opportunity in getting facts on behalf of the defence of this man.

Mr Clegg is perfectly aware what the evidence is that was given before the Coroner two years ago and I shall go very much on the evidence taken before the Coroner on that occasion. The prisoner, therefore, will be under no hardship.'

Mr Pollard also went on to complain that the entire hearing was unnecessary as he believed that the case should have been brought in front of the Assizes (now the Crown Court) without the need for a preliminary hearing, due to the conclusion of the Coroner, Mr Wightman, who had attributed the murder to Peace some two years earlier.

This was to be exactly the outcome of the hearing, and Peace was eventually remanded to appear before Leeds Assizes. The whole affair had been something of a non-event, an exercise in legal red tape, but did, however, produce some fascinating evidence, primarily due to the appearance in the witness box of the widowed Kate Dyson, who had very recently returned to Sheffield from visiting the United States.

Lifting her mourning veil to swear her oath and address the courtroom, she first confirmed her identity to the court, before recounting the unexpected housewarming appearance made at the family's new home in Banner Cross, just weeks before the night of her husband's tragic death:

'I am the widow of Arthur Dyson, and am now living at 58 Harrington Road, Sheffield. In 1876, I was living with my husband in Britannia Road, Darnall, and the prisoner lived next door to us. He was a picture-framer, and he framed four pictures for us.

He used to come to our house, but my husband did not like him, and asked him not to repeat his visits. He still continued to call, and in October, we removed from Darnall to Banner Cross. Some time prior to our removal, the prisoner came down the road, raised a pistol near to my face and said he should blow my brains out, and those of my husband.'

The threat at gunpoint was something which had not been discussed at the inquest two years before and cast a new, more sinister, light on the tormenting of the Dyson family at the hands of Peace. It is strange that this was never before revealed in public, as this was such a key part of the argument for the prosecution.

She went on to describe how Peace had made his unnerving appearance at their new premises, and confirmed that a warrant had been taken out against Peace in relation to the aforementioned threat.

'When I was going towards the house, I saw a man named Bolsover [Peace's future son-in-law] standing in the middle of the road. I walked over to Bolsover, knowing him to be on intimate terms with the prisoner, who was not there at that moment.

After speaking to him, I saw the prisoner coming out of the house where my goods were being taken into. We saw each other, and he said "You see, I am here to annoy you, wherever you go." I made the remark that I had a warrant for him, and he said he did not care for the warrant or the police either.'

The prosecution then asked Kate to recall the events of the night on which her husband was murdered. She spoke of the events exactly as she had done at the inquest into her husband's death, with very few variations from the exact wording she had used two years previously. The court chose not to interrupt her in her speech, as the events of the night had been well documented and studied meticulously by the court.

Another witness to make a return appearance at the proceedings was Mrs Sarah Colgrave, who chose this moment to embellish her tale of meeting Charles Peace on that fateful night, by revealing the full extent of the prisoner's crudeness during her conversation with him, and also revealing that she had herself played a key part in the events which led Peace to be returned to Sheffield and placed in the dock:

'I remember, about 7:30 on the evening of 29 November 1876, going to the shop of Mr Gregory. I met the prisoner thirty or forty yards from the shop. He asked me if I knew who lived in the second house; I told him no.

He said "Do you mind going and saying that an elderly gentleman wished to speak to her?" Again, I said no, and then he said," I will tell you, she's my bloody whore." I told him I thought he ought to mind what he said, especially to strangers. He then asked me to go with the message, and I said he had better go himself.

I left him and went on to Mr Gregory's shop. As I was leaving the shop ten minutes after, I saw the prisoner coming off the steps of the passage by the side of the house. He went up the road and I saw him no more, until I saw him in Newgate.'

THE SECOND JUDGEMENT

So, it would appear that it was Mrs Colgrave, a minor player in the events of the evening, who had, in fact, played a major role in identifying the fictional John Ward to be none other than the elusive Charles Frederick Peace. It would make sense that somebody who saw Peace on the night of the murder was taken to London to positively identify him, especially as Kate Dyson had been in America at the time of his arrest.

However, it also seems strange that a witness who had been unable to offer much of a description of the killer during the inquest into Arthur Dyson's death would have been selected to be the one who would travel at the expense of the authorities to make an identification. Be that as it may, Mrs Colgrave had certainly turned a walk-on part into a major Machiavellian role.

With no more part for the stipendiary magistrate and his colleagues to play, the case was committed to be heard before the Leeds Assizes. In a case of this magnitude, this would have been expected from the outset, and it would appear that the Sheffield proceedings were more of a symbolic gesture, forcing Peace to stand helplessly before his townsfolk and answer to the call of the law.

The trial and sentencing had been hastily arranged with Leeds Assizes, and it was less than a week later that Peace found himself in a much grander court of law. The civilian personnel were the same, the witnesses had travelled to West Yorkshire for the trial and the only changes were to the judge and counsel.

The services of the stipendiary magistrate had been dispensed with, only for him to be replaced by Mr Justice Lopes, a High Court Judge who carried with him a much more devastating arsenal of punishments than those available to the local magistrates (and who had, ironically, been one of the leading voices in the lobby to throw out the case against the Habron brothers in Manchester). Peace was now represented by the more sufficiently prepared Mr Lockwood, and Mr Campbell Foster appeared for the Crown.

By now apparently resigned to his dreadful fate, Peace had long given up any pretence of innocence, but maintained that the revolver had been discharged accidentally. All he wished for now was for a fair trial, and he certainly received a much more professional service before Judge Lopes.

The events which took place on the night of the murder had been discussed fully during the inquest and the committal in Sheffield and Mr Lopes chose to approach the case from a different angle. He knew *what* had happened and *where*, what he wanted to know was *how* and *why*?

After listening to Peace's version of events on the night in question, the Judge was interested to know how the prisoner had gone about escaping the long arm of the law. This had been, until now, a mystery to all involved. The only man who could fill in these gaps was Peace himself, and he was only too happy to describe his getaway.

'After that affair at Banner Cross, I went straight over the field opposite and through Endcliffe Wood to Crookes, and round by Sandygate. Then I doubled and came down to Broomhill, and there I took a cab and was driven down to the bottom of Church Street.

I got out and walked into Spring Street, to the house of an old pal. There I left my own clothes and disguised myself. I stopped there a short time, and then I went boldly through the streets to the railway station, and took a train for Rotherham. I walked from that station down to Masbro', where I took a ticket for Beverley.'

Mr Justice Lopes was keenly interested to find out how the prisoner had managed to create such a disguise that he remained at large for a matter of years, despite being one of the most wanted men in the country. The fascinating answer came from an account by one of Peace's jailers at Newgate (sadly unnamed) which had been given to a newspaper reporter.

'He said, "They talk about identifying me! Well, I could dodge any bobby living! I have dodged all the detectives in London many a time. I have walked past them, looked them straight in the face, and they thought I was a mulatto." Then he said to turn our faces away for a minute, and he would show us how he did it.

We turned our heads away, and when we looked again, we found that he had completely altered the expression of his countenance, and so entirely distorted and disfigured it, that he did not look like the same man. He threw out his under jaw, contracted the upper portion of his face, and appeared to be able to force the blood up into his head to give himself the appearance of a mulatto.'

The telling of this story in court no doubt caused Peace a rare smile in his time of judgement, as would the next item on the agenda. Kate Dyson was, once again, called to the witness box, but this time there would be no gentle touch or sympathetic questioning. The court, and the nation, wanted to know about the letters and notes found in a roll in the wake of Peace's escape.

Until this point the contents of the letters had remained undisclosed. Only the fact that they bore the prisoner's name and that they appeared to be in Mrs Dyson's handwriting had ever been revealed. The reading aloud of these notes must have been mortally embarrassing to the widow of the murdered man, but Peace, and his defence counsel, were determined that he would have his fair trial.

Judge Lopes allowed the contents of the notes to be read aloud to a packed courtroom. Whether these were of an embarrassing nature to the witness or not, the notes were evidence in a murder trial, and would be treated as such. They appear below as they appeared in the *Sheffield Evening Star* that very day, described in the newspaper as 'following the spelling and other eccentricities of the writer.'

'Do keep quiet. Don't let anyone see you. Money. Send me some.'
'Meet me in the Wicker, hope nothing will turn up to prevent it.'
'I will give you the wink when the coast is clear.'
'Give it to me in the garret, but don't talk for fear he is not going. Only his sister is coming. Love to all.'
'If you have a note for me, send it now while he is out, but you must not venture for he is watching Hope your foot is better, he went to Sheff yesterday, but I could not see you any where, were you out?'
'If you are not at home Janey will give you this, do be careful you will not get yourself in trouble about the empty house.'

In the grand scheme of the trial, these notes added very little to the facts and evidence on offer, but did shed new light on the relationship between Peace and Mrs Dyson. The notes do not suggest the neighbourly relationship as insisted by Kate, but rather an affair between the prisoner and a woman who was suspected of having drink and marital problems at the time.

It would also seem that the Dysons' housekeeper, an Irish immigrant known locally as Janey, was the go-between who had been tasked with the unenviable job of conveying these notes between the two parties. Also, as the contents of these notes remained unchallenged in court, it would also appear that the witness and the prosecution knew exactly what was in them, and had merely hoped that they would not be discussed to this degree.

However, even if taken at face value, the contents of the notes did not exonerate the prisoner in any way. If anything, it provided a cast-iron motive for his later actions. The mention of the 'empty house' also hints at Peace's habitual burglaries, and that Kate was well aware of his dark and criminal activities. However, further research reveals that the 'empty house' was the unoccupied house between their two homes, in which the couple would secretly meet.

All that remained to be decided was whether this was a case of cold-blooded murder, or if, as Peace maintained, the shooting was as a result of a struggle between the two men. Mr Lockwood put it to Kate Dyson that during the hearing at Sheffield, she had told the magistrate: '*I can't say my husband didn't get hold of the prisoner,*' to which the witness angrily responded: '*Put in the little word "try" please.*'

Kate Dyson was not to be swayed on her testimony that her husband did not manage to get hold of Peace, but had made an attempt to do so. As the sole witness to the events of those few moments, her statement had to be believed and from this point the first nail had been hammered into the casket of Charles Peace.

The second nail was delivered by the return of Charles Brassington, who repeated his testimony from the inquest and the preliminary hearing, in which he solemnly confirmed that, during a conversation with him outside the Banner Cross Hotel, Peace *had* threatened to shoot the couple.

A further blow to the defence came in the way of the newly discovered science of forensics, during which it was revealed to the court that the revolver, recovered from the possession of Peace during his arrest in London, bore the same rifling as the bullet which had been removed from the brain of Arthur Dyson.

THE SECOND JUDGEMENT

The game was up. The only course of action left to the defence was to plead for the life of the prisoner. During his closing speech, Mr Lockwood twice implored the jury to be lenient with his client, as he 'was in such a state of wickedness as to be quite unprepared to face death'. This bizarre reasoning was also met with an equally bizarre response from Peace, who raised his eyes to the heavens and howled 'I am not fit to die!'

During his summing up, Mr Justice Lopes dismissed the theory of the accidental shooting as an 'absolute surmise', even going as far as inviting the members of the jury to try and pull the stiff trigger of the revolver as if 'accidentally'. He also reminded the jury of the forensic report which linked this gun to the bullet removed from the skull of the victim.

Aware of the distress caused to Kate Dyson during the reading of the notes between herself and Peace, the judge admitted that it was perfectly reasonable for Mr Lockwood to have wanted to discredit the testimony of Mrs Dyson, but added that the case did not rest on one testimony. The threats towards the Dysons had been confirmed by other witnesses.

A weak interjection by Mr Lockwood that the other witnesses could have been paid to corroborate the story was quickly and angrily dismissed by Mr Lopes, who had by now heard quite enough of this sordid affair. It was his opinion that no struggle had taken place to cause the revolver to fire 'accidentally', and that the defence had no further grounds for argument.

By this stage of proceedings, it was after seven o'clock in the evening, and the Judge ordered the jury to retire and 'do their duty to the community at large, and by the oath that they each had sworn'. It was a mere ten minutes before they returned with their verdict.

Upon receiving the verdict, and before passing sentence, Mr Justice Lopes had asked the prisoner if he had anything to say. 'It's no use my saying anything,' came the resigned and defeated reply of a man who had been finally brought to justice after evading the law for so long. The defiant spark in the heart of Charles Frederick Peace was about to be permanently extinguished.

'Then, I will not aggravate the situation with a recapitulation of any portion of the details of what I fear, I may call your criminal career,' replied Mr Justice Lopes, before donning the black cap and passing down the only sentence fit for an habitual criminal and confirmed murderer.

Peace was sentenced to hang for his crimes.

Chapter 13

Prepare for Eternity, Charlie Peace

'Death is a great revealer of what is in a man, and in its solemn
shadow appear the naked lineaments of the soul.'
E.H Chapin, Journalist and Preacher, 1841-1880

Defeated and condemned, Peace was taken from court and transported under heavy guard on the short journey between Leeds Assizes and Armley Gaol. This was to be his place of execution and it was to be in his home county that he would spend the final days of his wretched and eventful life.

Leeds Prison, known locally as Armley Gaol, is one of the best examples one could wish to find of an archetypal nineteenth century prison. Ominous and foreboding, this was to be the last port of call for many a Victorian villain, as this was the place where executioners were charged with a duty to exact the ultimate punishment upon those who had been found guilty of grievous wrongdoing in the county of Yorkshire.

Built to resemble an impressive medieval castle, and to instil the fear of God into those who looked upon its high walls and narrow windows, the prison opened its twin-towered gates in 1847. Purpose built to house the most dangerous criminals in the area, Armley Gaol had, in 1864, taken the solemn mantle of carrying out executions from the, by this time, largely defunct York Castle.

All in all, the prison carried out ninety-four executions between 1864 and 1961, almost one per year. However, from these ninety-four executions, some famously gruesome tales were born.

The original hangman at Armley Gaol was Thomas Askern, an experienced executioner who had previously plied his trade in his native York. Of the many executions over which he was to preside, only one was held publically, such were the changes in the law around this time.

This was the double execution of convicted killers James Sargisson and Joseph Myers.

The two were being executed for unrelated crimes, but had formed a friendship during their imprisonment. Sargisson had been found guilty of murdering a man during the course of a robbery in Rotherham, just a few miles from the hometown of Charlie Peace, where he had pursued a stranger into the countryside with the intention of stealing his expensive watch.

Myers, a local man from the outskirts of Leeds, had been found guilty of murdering his wife with a pair of scissors. With a long history of alcoholism and violence, his claim that he had acted whilst under the effect of a seizure had been dismissed by the courts.

Almost 100,000 people travelled to Leeds that Saturday morning to witness the end of two such wicked men and to their delight, just before 9am, the two murderers were brought to the gallows. Placed side by side and hooded, their last words were to each other, with Sargisson asking Myers: 'Art thou happy lad?' to which his partner in death replied: 'Indeed I am.'

Myers certainly wasn't happy, having previously made an attempt to deliver his own fate by cutting his own throat just days before the execution, but the suicide attempt was discovered and the prisoner saved by the in-house doctor. Myers would not have long to wait before meeting his maker.

The two men dropped simultaneously as the lever was pulled. Myers died instantly, but it was reported that the stronger Sargisson took almost five minutes to become still at the end of his rope. Luckily, most of the drama was hidden from the crowd by the wooden construction which housed the trapdoors.

Sargisson's drawn-out death was not the only unplanned event of that day, with the unfortunate, yet inevitable, reopening of Myers' throat wound upon being suspended by the neck, causing a large amount of blood to flow from beneath the noose and onto his shirt. Baying crowd or not, it does seem fortunate that the assembled onlookers were spared this appallingly grim spectacle.

This was not to be the only botched execution during the tenure of Thomas Askern, with *'a shocking scene'* being reported some thirteen years later during the hanging of John Henry Johnson, who had been convicted of murdering a rival for his wife's affections during a long and debauched Boxing Day drinking session in 1877.

As usual, Askern made his way to Leeds on the day of the execution, and quickly performed his checks before sending for the condemned man. However, it would appear that Askern's preparations were not as thorough as usual. Everything had gone to plan, right until the moment the lever was pulled.

The very second that the trapdoor opened and the rope took the full weight of its load, there was a load snap, and the rope broke like a piece of cheap string. Johnson plummeted over ten feet to the ground, as the assembled warders dashed, somewhat ironically, to his assistance.

Johnson was seated in a chair, with his hood and pinions removed, until Askern managed to rig the gallows once more. This time, the rope held fast, and Johnson had been unfortunate enough to enjoy only minutes of his unexpected reprieve.

No official blame was ever attributed to Askern or his tools; indeed, the incident was conveniently left out of the subsequent execution report. However, gossip in relation to this horrifc incident spread like wildfire, and as such, somebody in high places must have been deeply unimpressed by this amateurish affair, as Thomas Askern was never to pull the lever at Armley again.

He was eventually replaced by a man who stood by his work, and prided himself on never having caused any unnecessary suffering. This was a hangman who was later to share some tender moments with one especially notorious criminal, and whose poignant words on one particularly fateful day would be recorded for posterity.

This notorious criminal was, of course, Charlie Peace, who now languished in a small, bare, prison cell, reserved for only the most wicked of characters. He had seen much of the country during his villainous escapades, but as fate would have it, his last home was to be the condemned prisoner's cell at Armley Gaol.

His first days as a condemned man were as melancholy and silent as the cell itself. Peace refused any interaction with his guards and turned down visiting requests from his friends and family, of which there were many. It would seem that the brazen burglar and callous killer had become every inch the petulant child, sitting in silence and brooding over his punishment.

Fortunately for all involved, Peace began to revert to his gregarious self after a few days of wallowing in self pity. It would seem that he had taken notice of some advice given by the very man who had ordered his imprisonment and execution, none other than the judge, Mr Justice Lopes.

'Prepare for eternity, Charles Peace' had been the sound advice delivered during the closing moments of his trial. There was to be no escape this time: this was the end, and the only chance of salvation the wretched inhabitant of the dock had was to make his peace with himself, his loved ones, and with God.

With hours of time to fill each day, but every day leading to his death, Peace began to ponder on his misspent life. He thought about the family he was to leave behind, the victims who left behind their own families, and of course, his failings as a master criminal in being caught by something as simple as a good old act of treachery.

Ironically, Peace had expressed a wish to be visited by Susan Gray, the very woman who had betrayed him. One can only guess whether this was for the purpose of delivering a few choice words, or of granting forgiveness, the way only a man about to meet his maker can. Sensibly, he accepted the wishes of his family that he was not to see 'that woman' for the short remainder of his life.

Having been on the receiving end of the law herself, due to her involvement with Peace, his wife was surprisingly eager to see her condemned husband. This was certainly a woman who took her wedding vows seriously, and after standing by Peace throughout his involvement with Susan Gray, and allegedly, Kate Dyson, there can certainly be no question as to her undying loyalty to the man with whom she had wished to spend the rest of her life.

The Peace family began to hold daily visits, where they would pray, sing, and talk about the old times. This was the wholesome family life that had always been available to Charlie Peace, but sadly had been blindly rejected in favour of a life of crime and debauchery.

By now resigned to his fate, Peace had thought in depth about his relationship with Susan Gray, and decided that he could bear no grudge towards her. Heeding the warnings of his newly reunited family, he wrote a note of forgiveness, and asked another regular visitor to deliver it into the hands of his former lover.

Henry Brion had visited Peace in both Newgate and Armley Gaols. However, his visits were largely in his own interests, as the inventions drawn up by himself and Peace bore both names on their patents, and with Peace having conned his former co-inventor with a fabricated identity, Brion felt it only fair that he solely owned the patents, if anything, to make up for the damage to his reputation caused by his former friend.

At first, Peace flatly refused to remove his (false) name from the patents unless Brion could come up with £50, which would then be given to the soon to be fatherless Peace family. There was to be no such deal, Brion would not pay for the rights to his own inventions, and made this clear on each visit.

Eventually, with salvation and godliness on his mind, Peace relented with grace and goodwill, saying: 'Very well my friend, let it be as you say. I have not cheated you, heaven knows. But I also know this infamy of mine has been the cause of bringing harm to you, which is the last thing I should have wished to cause to my friend.'

A contract was quickly drawn up by Brion, which gave him sole ownership of the pair's inventions, and was signed by Charlie Peace, alias John Thompson, alias John Ward. The deed was done, and Henry Brion had all he wanted from his former friend. Brion quickly took his leave, and promised to visit again, but, sadly, for the second time, had no intention of doing so.

Before exiting through the imposing prison gates, Brion had asked to see the prison governor, and during the short meeting he was granted, implored that the amount of guards responsible for keeping Peace captive be doubled, as his former friend's repentance was nothing more than 'bunkum', and that he had 'considerable anxiety for the public good' should Peace be left alone for a second.

Perhaps this betrayal was a product of fear; Brion had persistently badgered Peace, and in doing so, forced the hand of a notorious killer, one with a known talent for escape. Nobody knew the level of Peace's ingenuity more comprehensively than Brion, and surely a man who could invent a mechanism for raising sunken ships could invent a means of escaping a prison, given the slightest opportunity.

Clutching the signed paperwork closely to his chest and heading quickly back to his native London, Brion was not to be seen at Armley Gaol again. Indeed, his talents as a solo inventor in the aftermath of Peace's incarceration seem to be so ineffectual that he was largely unheard of again for the rest of his career, with no further inventions of note being credited to him.

Despite the inventor's misgivings, it would appear that Peace by now was a man set upon atonement and his own spiritual wellbeing, as shortly after seeing the back of Brion for the last time, Peace received another visitor, one who would be instrumental in helping Peace to finalise his repentance, and make his peace with God.

Mr Littlewood was the vicar of Darnall, Sheffield, the place in which Peace had so desperately wanted to be buried and the place he considered, above all, to be his home. Littlewood and Peace had known each other for a number of years, as the former had acted as Chaplain at nearby Wakefield Prison during one of Peace's earlier incarcerations.

In his letters to Littlewood, penned just a few days after receiving his sentence, Peace had expressed a wish to put right his life of wrongdoing, and informed his former acquaintance that the confession he wished to make would bring not only his own atonement, but that of others. There was only one victim of Peace's wrongdoings who could be saved, and this act of salvation was to be started as a matter of urgency.

Having asked Littlewood to accompany him in meeting with the prison governor, the vicar's first duty as a trusted man of the cloth was to witness a rare piece of honesty from Peace, who began to tell a tale to the two men, one of murder, escape, and wrongful conviction. It was time for the record to be put straight on the tragic murder of Constable Cock.

The governor listened intently to the story which was laid out before him, and conferred with Mr Littlewood as to his views on the validity of Peace's late confession to this heinous crime. Both were suitably convinced that Peace knew all of the ins and outs of the case, but harboured a small doubt that Peace was simply using his impending death as a means to free one of his past criminal cohorts.

The unfortunate Willian Habron had languished in prison since the fateful events at Whalley Range, despite his continuing protests of innocence. He was certainly no friend of Charlie Peace and Peace only knew of the man who had carried the blame for his own crimes due to his heartless attendance at the trial of the innocent young man.

Knowing that innocence must be proven as much as guilt in a case of this kind, the governor knew he had to be sure of Peace's version of events, and as such, provided paper and ink for his prisoner to create a detailed confession, including drawings and plans of the crime scene and his escape route.

The confession detailed the empty house at Whalley Range, which was the intended location of a burglary, and the actual location of a murder. Peace described how he had worn respectable clothes during his stay in Greater Manchester as this, he maintained, made it easier to be ignored by the local police.

He described in detail the events which took place on the night of the murder: that he had been about to gain entry to the empty house when he had heard a rustle in the bushes behind him and saw the silhouette of a policeman approaching. In desperation, he had quickly fled the scene and climbed a wall, only to land within feet of another constable.

Constable Cock had turned at the sound of Peace's footsteps, and begun to approach. Maintaining that he had given a warning to the young constable, Peace described how he had fired a shot wide of Cock, but was force to shoot again as the brave young man continued his approach.

'These Manchester policemen are a very obstinate lot' remarked Peace; as he went on to describe where the bullet hit his victim, and how he had immediately fled across the fields to safety before making a circuitous journey back to Hull and the unknowing embrace of his family. However, it was not long before he crossed the Pennines again.

Peace had read of the arrest of the Habron brothers in a newspaper and, despite his underlying misgivings, could not resist attending the trial. After a flying visit to his native Sheffield, he had made the journey to Manchester Assizes to watch the trial and sentencing of an innocent man, offering only a half-hearted justification of his heartless actions:

'People will say that I am a hardened wretch for allowing an innocent man to suffer for the crime for which I was guilty, but what man would have given himself up under such circumstances, knowing, as I did, that I should certainly be hanged?'

PREPARE FOR ETERNITY, CHARLIE PEACE

The details, of course, matched the official reports to a tee, and it was now the duty of the governor to inform the Home Secretary that an error of the very worst kind had been made, and that an innocent man must be freed in one of the most high profile murder cases the north of England had ever seen. There were going to be repercussions, and only immediate action could begin to spare the blushes of the British courts.

After almost three years of hard labour and imprisonment, William Habron was quietly freed from prison, no official statements were ever made and no blame was ever aimed at anyone in authority over the case. He was given a free pardon, and granted the princely sum of £500 in a closed session of Parliament. In Victorian England this was easily enough for a man to disappear and begin a comfortable new life.

Once reunited with his brothers, the three chose to take the money and return to their native Ireland, with no further mention of the gross miscarriage of justice being made in Parliament or the press. The British justice system had managed to emerge relatively unscathed from this scandal, especially as they now knew for certain the identity of the real killer.

With the business of the Habron case taken care of, Peace had only one item left on his agenda: to make every possible effort to save his own wretched soul. Again, Mr Littlewood found himself in an audience with Peace, just days before his execution. This time the two men would be alone, as this was to be a private and emotional affair between a man of God and an habitual criminal.

Having spent weeks in a cold cell in the harsh British winter, Peace was suffering from influenza, but warmly greeted the vicar with the words: 'I am very poorly sir, but exceedingly pleased to see you', to which his visitor assured the prisoner that he had every sympathy for him, and would do everything he could to unburden the shivering inmate before him.

At this, Peace broke down in tears. He was not accustomed to such sympathy and asked Mr Littlewood to believe in the truth and sincerity of the confession he was about to make. He had accepted his fate and his culpability in the crimes for which he was to hang. Finally, a feeling of humanity had fallen upon the soul of Charlie Peace.

'If I could undo, or make amends for anything I have done, I would suffer my body as I stand now to be cut in piece inch by inch. I feel, sir, that I am too bad to live or die, and having this feeling I cannot think that either you or anyone else would believe me, and that is the reason why I ask you so much to try to be assured that you do not think I am telling lies. I call God to witness that all I am saying, and wish to say, will be the truth...nothing but the truth.'

To Mr Littlewood's great surprise, the matter which seemed to be playing the most heavily on the mind of the confessor was not one of murder; it was not even one of habitual burglary. It was the worry of being blamed for a small crime which had occurred some years before, which had been attributed to Peace, but was a misdemeanour he vehemently denied.

It would seem that, during one of his stays in Darnall, a clock had gone missing from the day school of the church at which Mr Littlewood held office. Due to his reputation, the blame had been firmly laid upon Peace, but as this was such a small crime, no action had ever been taken. It would appear however, that amidst the burglary and murder of his career, this was one crime which troubled Peace.

The vicar admitted that he himself had believed Peace to have stolen the clock, but found the whole matter to be of small consequence in the greater scheme of things. However, with sincerity and rare honesty, Peace maintained that he did not take the clock and would have been more likely to have *bought* a clock for the church such was his respect for Mr Littlewood.

Pausing for a moment, Littlewood replied 'Peace, I am convinced now that you did not take the clock. I cannot believe that you dare deny it now in your position, if you really did.' At this, Peace admitted to knowing that some colliers he knew had taken the clock, but such is the unwritten code of the criminal world, did not make this known at the time. With this, he broke down in tears once again.

Upon regaining his composure, it was time to turn their attention to the matters for which he was now facing execution: the harassment and murder of Arthur Dyson. Having been satisfied that the vicar now believed in his ability to tell the truth, Peace began to give his version of the unfortunate series of events which occurred on that terrible night in Banner Cross.

He strongly maintained his claims that his relationship with Kate Dyson had been far from the innocent friendship described by the widow in court, claims that were certainly aided by the revelation of the contents of the letters sent between the two, and that he had travelled to Banner Cross to ask Mrs Dyson to persuade her husband to withdraw the warrant taken out against him.

Rather than having accosted Kate as she left the outside privy, Peace claimed to have approached her in the yard of her home in an attempt to speak to her quietly and privately, but was greeted with violent and threatening language and in an attempt to suppress the commotion had taken out his revolver which he then held to her head.

He maintained that he had warned her to be quiet, but she failed to take heed of his warning. It was at this point that Arthur Dyson emerged from the back door of the house, and immediately began angrily to approach Peace. Being only too aware of the warrant against him, Peace stated that he had begun to run away from the oncoming threat and make his way along the passageway towards Banner Cross Road.

As he had always maintained, Peace reiterated that Arthur Dyson had caught up with him and the two were involved in a struggle at the foot of the steps onto the main road. This was also mentioned by Kate Dyson in an early statement, but was later changed to insist that Peace had shot at her husband as he approached.

During the struggle, Peace claimed that the revolver had been fired to the side of the two men, but Dyson had not loosened his grip in response. It was at this point that Peace knew he had to make every attempt to get away and managed to free his arm sufficiently to take the only course of action available to him.

'I had not a moment to spare. I made a desperate effort, wrenched the arm from him and fired again. All that was in my head at the time was to get away. I never did intend, either there or anywhere else, to take a man's life; but I was determined that I should not be caught at that time, as the result, knowing what I had done

143

before, would have been worse even than had I stayed under the warrant.'

Peace also asserted that, had he wished to murder Arthur Dyson, he would have found a better way of doing this than in the middle of a public street. He also stressed his belief that Kate Dyson had been guilty of the most serious perjury, having denied that the shot was fired during a violent struggle.

The versions of events as told by the only two witnesses differ only slightly, but it is these minor differences that speak volumes about the intentions of Charlie Peace. In Kate Dyson's version, he is a cold-blooded killer who turned to shoot an unarmed man, and in his own version, he was a man who had acted desperately in a violent struggle.

However, even taking into consideration Peace's story, this did certainly not absolve him of guilt; it merely suggested that the murder had no premeditation. This, coupled with the murder of Constable Cock, had left the repentant Peace with no doubt that he deserved the noose which would soon be placed around his neck.

He asked Mr Littlewood to pray with him, and invited his two guards to join them in praying for his soul, which they duly did. For twenty minutes this convicted murderer led the small group in a prayer, described by those present as fluent and earnest. He asked for blessing upon his victims and their families, and prayed for the future of his own family.

Upon finishing the prayer, Peace asked of Mr Littlewood whether he should ask Kate Dyson to visit in order to ask her for forgiveness, to which the clergyman responded that Peace should save his remaining energy for asking the forgiveness of God.

Peace nodded his agreement, and thanked those present for joining him in prayer. He wished Mr Littlewood a safe journey home, before struggling to rise to his feet in his weakened condition. The two guards solemnly lifted their prisoner onto his bed, and as he turned to face the wall, he began to weep uncontrollably.

Chapter 14

Mr Marwood's Rope

'Lion-hearted I've lived.
And when my time comes, lion-hearted I'll die.'
Charles Peace, Murderer and Burglar, 1832-1879

For centuries the sharp end of British justice had been administered by resident executioners who operated at their local prison and, in return, were paid a salary for their services. Many such hangmen had inherited their position from their forefathers and were indoctrinated into this macabre profession without any kind of royal, or government, approval.

Every prison in which these men plied their trade had some kind of sinister tale to tell, whether it be the story of a botched execution at the hands of a drunken hangman, or an account of an unnecessarily violent end to the life of a convict. In short, rumours of corruption and complacency were commonplace after almost every execution.

Having already abolished the cruel and gruesome circus of public executions some years earlier, by the 1870s, the government were becoming increasingly squeamish about capital punishment. Gone were the days of drunken crowds baying for the blood of the condemned; it was time for this deeply unpleasant duty to be carried out privately, quietly and methodically.

The world was changing, and any such violent unpleasantness was now to be swept beneath a carpet of gentility. An air of respectability was needed to improve the image of the British justice system and this meant disposing of the desensitised and unlicensed local executioners. They were to be replaced by men of learning and moral standing, men who could ensure that such a difficult task could be carried out without controversy or error.

The rapid expanse of the British rail system now ensured that no execution required the services of a local hangman; it was simpler, more cost effective and more *proper* to create a handful of licensed executioners who were able to attend any part of the country by rail and carry out their scheduled duty by royal appointment.

One of the first men to bring scientific knowledge and quiet efficiency to the role of executioner was William Marwood, a cobbler from rural Lincolnshire, who had long studied both the physics and the morality of sending a convict to his death at the gallows. However, at the age of 54, he had still yet to perform, or even assist in, a real execution.

Armed with his considerable knowledge of science and evidence of his studies, Marwood was certain that he could bring in new developments which would improve efficiency in the art of hanging. So much so, that he had approached the governor of Lincoln prison with his research and asked permission to carry out an execution without pay in order to prove his credibility.

It does seem strange that this was immediately agreed to by the prison governor, but in those days of penal reform, and with a need for quiet and respectable executions, it would seem that Marwood's well-researched methods were given the chance he had asked for; after all, what did anyone have to lose?

Marwood was given his chance on 1 February 1872 when he was tasked with the hanging of William Frederick Horry, a husband and father from nearby Boston, who had fatally shot his wife whilst in a jealous rage. Having met his executioner prior to his death, and being in no position to protest, Horry was led to the gallows by a novice hangman.

Having expertly assessed the mechanism of the trapdoor and calculated the amount of rope needed to ensure a quick death, Marwood showed no nerves or emotion as he pulled the lever that sent William Horry to meet his maker; he trusted in his abilities, and knew for sure that no man would suffer pain by his hand.

The sight which instantly greeted the prison officials was nothing more than a taut, still rope. Not even the tiniest movement could be detected. There was also silence - none of the choking or convulsing which had often added extra unpleasantness to such proceedings could be heard. Horry's death had been instantaneous.

The reason for the adulation and warm congratulations which followed had been Marwood's tireless studies of a method of hanging often used in Ireland. It was known as the long drop, and would from this day onwards, until the abolition of capital punishment, be the standard method of execution by hanging.

Based simply around a calculation of the condemned man's height and weight, and the placement of the knot, pulled tightly behind the left ear before releasing the trapdoor, this new method ensured that the cause of death would be an instant breaking of the neck due to the longer length of rope, rather than the agonising moments of suffocation which had haunted many of those who had been unfortunate enough to witness a botched execution.

Having proved his worth in a handful of subsequent hangings, just two years later Marwood was appointed by the Sheriffs of London and Middlesex as an official hangman of the state, and was given a £20 per annum retainer along with £10 per execution. He did, however, maintain his career as a cobbler but took pride in hanging a sign which read 'Marwood Crown Office' above the door of his humble business.

During his career, Marwood would oversee the execution of 179 people and his services would be requested as far afield as Ireland, Scotland, and Jersey. Many notable murderers and villains were to meet their end in the presence of this professional and capable state executioner, but the most famous of all Marwood's hangings would require just a relatively short trip from Lincolnshire to West Yorkshire.

Tuesday 25 February 1879 had been decided upon as the day Charlie Peace would hang and, such was the public interest in this case, every national newspaper announced this date to its readers. Peace, despite his captivity, was still something of a celebrity and as such his name was to be heard in churches and meeting rooms around the country, his deeds and eventual punishment used as a deterrent for any person who threatened to stray from the path of righteousness.

In Peace's hometown of Sheffield, a sermon was read by a Dr Potter, in which he warned of the temptations of crime and debauchery, assuring his congregation that 'All hope of Peace's salvation is gone forever.' When news of this reached Peace in his cell, so certain was he that his soul could be saved that he responded 'Well...Mr Potter may think so, but I don't.'

It is this mood of repentance and search for moral salvation that greeted all who visited Peace in his final days. Although still suffering terribly from the influenza that left him shivering and weak, there was work still to be done to ensure his passage into heaven and to this end he devoted most of his remaining time to his long-suffering family.

On the Saturday before his execution, Peace was visited by his brother and sister-in-law along with their two children. Although emotional and full of regret, he spoke with bravery as to the events which would greet him just three days later, hoping that this stoic show of acceptance would diminish the sense of sadness felt by his loved ones.

He described how he would die at around 8am, and that by 4pm an inquest would be held upon his corpse. Describing the bleak, pitiful funeral that would be held for him in which his body would be lowered into an unmarked grave without blessing or fond words, he asked one small favour of his family: that they each place a flower in a small graveyard near Darnall, Sheffield, on the day of his execution.

Before his visitors took their leave of him, Peace took his brother, Daniel, aside and warned him of the consequences of 'bad living', begging him to 'become religious', and not to follow in the villainous footsteps of his own condemned brother. However, the warning was not met with great enthusiasm and Daniel left his brother's side for the last time furious at any comparison Charlie had made between the two of them.

However, despite this awkward parting, the family left the grounds of the prison in tears; this had been an emotional meeting, and their day was about to become a little more difficult as they came face to face with another of Peace's loved ones upon reaching the street outside the imposing, towered gates.

Pacing the pavement, and waiting tirelessly for any news of her former lover, was Susan Gray, the woman who had betrayed Peace for financial gain. Approaching the family, she desperately attempted to assure them of her remorse and guilt for the events which had led to them saying a final farewell to a member of their family.

Having been reassured that these family members at least, bore no grudge, and wished her no malice, the former 'Nottingham Nightingale' begged for news of her 'Dear John', still fondly clinging to the pseudonym by which she had known, and fallen in love with, her soon to be departed former lover. The news which came was blunt and matter-of-fact, such was the Peace's family way.

The family told Susan of how they had found Peace to be 'a poor, wretched and haggard man' due to his illness and current predicament and that Peace had no wish to see her for the short remainder of his life. Susan broke down in tears and it was at this point that Daniel led his family away to undertake their journey back to Sheffield; he was never to see his brother again.

The next day was a Sunday, so no visitors were permitted, even to a condemned man. Sunday was a day for prayer and worship, and Peace certainly wished to spend his day bringing himself one step closer to salvation. This was also the day that William Marwood arrived in Leeds; ready to begin his meticulous preparations the following morning.

The last full day of Peace's life arrived, and with it came a visit from his wife, daughter and son-in-law. Before the visitors had even had a chance to embrace him, Peace asked his visitors to keep their emotions in check. He was in good spirits, and did not wish to be overcome by emotion during the final hours of his life.

Aware of the financial hardship that his death would impose upon his family, Peace made a list of his belongings and creations, which could be sold for much needed income. He had made a living from depriving people of their own valuables, so it was only fair and just that his own possessions be sold for profit.

Peace had also, some years before, created a drawing of a monument which was to adorn his own grave. This was also given to his family, in the hope that, one day, there would be some kind of memorial to his life, apart from the unmarked grave within the precincts of the prison into which his cheap coffin would be unceremoniously lowered.

As during the visit of his brother just days before, Peace began to describe the events of his forthcoming execution, reassuring his weeping wife that he had no fear of death, as he was confident that he had been successful in atoning for his sins. However, at this point, he fell silent, listening to a muffled sound in the distance.

'That's a noise that would make some men fall to the floor" he said quietly 'They are working at my own scaffold.' The two warders who were tasked to accompany Peace at all times quickly denied that this was the case, but Peace replied 'I have not worked so long with wood that I don't know the sound of deals [a term used for a type of wood]; and they don't have deals inside a prison for anything else than scaffolds.'

Horrified by the indignity of the situation, Hannah Peace asked for the work to be stopped until the visit was over, but the condemned man assured all present that the noise did not upset him, he had made his peace, and he was not afraid to die. This appears to have been one of the only glitches in the otherwise entirely conscientious preparations of an execution under the guidance of William Marwood.

Undeterred by the sound of his impending fate, Peace admitted that his body would be 'treated with scant ceremony after his death', but knew that by this point his soul would be welcomed into heaven, leaving behind only the wretched corpse of a former sinner.

Despite his earlier protestations, by the time the visit ended, Peace, and his family were in tears. Keen to put right his neglect of his family during previous years, he asked them if there was anything more they wished of him before his death. Hannah Peace reminded her husband that he had promised to join them in prayer.

Never in his life had Peace been so willing to pray and the small group knelt together for another half an hour, with Peace praying for every member of his family and encouraging them to pray for him, and for one another. When the prayers were concluded, Peace was once again reduced to tears and shook hands with each of his family members, pausing to hand a self-penned memorial card to his wife, which read:

'In Memory of Charles Peace who was executed in Armley Prison Tuesday February 25th, 1879, Aged 47
For that I don but never intended [sic]'

As Peace had suspected, and his warders denied, just a few walls away from the condemned cell stood the proud instigator of the long drop, thoughtfully gazing upon the scaffold which was currently being hastily erected to his own detailed designs.

MR MARWOOD'S ROPE

Had Mr Marwood been aware of the fact that these labours could be heard by the condemned man, he would certainly have been annoyed that his professional standards had been called into question, but as for pity for the man who would soon climb the scaffold by his side, he would have none - Marwood was a man who held his duties in high regard, later quoted as saying;

'I am doing God's work according to the divine command and the law of the British Crown. I do it simply as a matter of duty and as a Christian. I sleep as soundly as a child and am never disturbed by phantoms. Where there is guilt there is bad sleeping, but I am conscious that I try to live a blameless life.

Detesting idleness, I pass my vacant time in and work in my shoe shop near the church day after day until such time as I am required elsewhere. It would have been better for those I executed if they had preferred industry to idleness.'

However, in a few short hours, he was to meet a man who was to challenge his views on criminality, and those who stood over the trapdoor, waiting for their end to come. William Marwood would never meet another man like the character he would lead up those wooden steps the very next morning.

There was never a moment in Peace's life where he could have been compared to royalty. That is, until the bitterly cold morning of his execution arrived. In conversation with his warders as he dressed, Peace remarked to them that like his namesake, King Charles I, he hoped the cold would not cause him to shiver on the scaffold, as he did not wish onlookers to believe he was trembling in fear.

Such staunch belief in his eternal salvation, coupled with his innate bravery, had made Peace a popular prisoner amongst his warders, and an air of sadness could be felt amongst those who had been charged to watch over this unique, intriguing little man. He was allowed to spend his final hours eating heartily, and writing letters his friends and family.

Despite his illness, Peace was in high spirits, although he appeared a little thoughtful when it was announced that the executioner would soon

151

be arriving to take him to the scaffold. However, the thoughts that were playing on his mind were not about his death, they were simply pangs of fear that he would die in pain.

Banishing the troublesome thoughts from his head, Peace went into a coughing fit, and joked with his warders: 'I wonder if Mr Marwood can cure this cough of mine?' This little joke once again lifted Peace's mood, and it was only the arrival of the executioner that removed the mischievous smile from his lips.

He had asked to be allowed a few moments with Mr Marwood, as he wished to speak to him briefly before being taken from the cell. His thoughts about the pain of execution had once again arisen, and he sought reassurance that he would not suffer.

Taking the hangman to one side, Peace said: 'I hope you will not punish me. I hope you will do your work quickly' to which Marwood replied: 'You shall not suffer pain from my hand.' This was enough for Peace as he shook hands with his hangman and immediately turned to address those present in his cell and offer his blessings:

'God bless you, I hope to meet you all in heaven. I am thankful to say my sins are all forgiven.'

Without fuss or reluctance, Peace allowed himself to be prepared for his fate. He remained calm throughout the preparations, even engaging in conversation with one of the warders as his restraints were fitted. Never in his career had William Marwood witnessed such brave acceptance of impending death.

As he was led from his cell and into the execution area, Peace did allow his impenetrable stoicism to slip momentarily, faltering slightly as the gallows came in sight. However, he soon regained his composure and climbed the stair unaided, apart from Marwood's hand upon his shoulder to ensure that he did not fall on the stairs.

Standing upon the scaffold, and looking out upon those who had been admitted to his execution, Peace, who had previously declined to allow himself any final words, asked Marwood to stop as he was about to place the hood over his head, saying that he wished to speak to the members of the press who had been invited to attend.

'You gentlemen reporters, I wish you to notice the few words I am going to say. You know what my life has been. It has been base; but I wish you to notice, for the sake of others, how a man can die, as I am about to die, in fear of the Lord.

Gentlemen, my heart says that I feel assured that my sins are forgiven me, that I am going to the Kingdom of Heaven, or else to the place prepared for those who rest until the great Judgment day.

I do not think I have any enemies, but if there are any who would be so, I wish them well. Gentlemen, all and all, I wish them to come to the Kingdom of Heaven when they die, as I am going to die.'

Thinking of his family in his final moments, Peace concluded his speech by pleading that he did not wish anyone to think badly of them, or for them to suffer on his behalf.

'I hope no-one will disgrace them by taunting them or jeering them on my account, but to have mercy upon them. God bless you, my dear children. Goodbye, and Heaven bless you. Amen. Oh, my Lord God, have mercy upon me!'

With that, the hood was finally placed over his head and in a manner akin to the sharpness of his earlier self, Peace demanded a drink of water, and repeated his demand when it was denied. Repentant and remorseful or not, Peace would die as he lived - making mischief and refusing to be denied anything.

Mr Marwood pulled the lever, and the trapdoor created to his own design swung open with all of the smoothness one would expect from such a master of his craft. And with that, there was silence; only the creaking of the rope which descended from view into the faultlessly built structure could be heard.

Peace had died instantly; Mr Marwood was as good as his word.

This may have been the only occasion in history where a world without Peace was a better place.

Having dedicated his life to the suffering of others, it is perhaps fitting that an obituary to Charles Frederick Peace is not lovingly created from the sentimental writings of his friends or family, but is taken from the words of William Marwood, the man who finally rid the world of an habitual criminal responsible for the deaths of two unfortunate men.

The following is taken from an interview with the *Sheffield and Rotherham Independent* in the days immediately following the execution of Charles Peace.

'Before his execution, he said to one of the warders "Do you think Mr Marwood can cure this bad cough of mine?" The warder replied "I have no doubt he could" And I can tell you, that a man who jokes about getting hanged to cure a cough is no coward.

A firmer step never walked to the scaffold. I admired his bravery; he met his fate like a man; he acknowledged his guilt, and his hope in God with regard to his future was very good.

During the seven years I have officiated as executioner, I have never met a man who faced death with greater calmness. The bravery was the outcome of his nature, he was ignorant alike of weakness or timidity.'

Epilogue:

Peace by Peace

'The only interesting criminals are those worthy of something better. Peace was one of these. If his life may be said to point a moral, it is the very simple one that crime is no career for a man of brains.'
H B Irving, British Stage Actor and Author, 1870-1919

Crookes, Sheffield, 1 October 2015.
As I sit alone in my little home office, reeling from the realisation that my work is almost complete, it has become something of an enigma to me as to how to *feel* about the man whose incredible story has dominated the last nine months of my life.

There can be no doubt that Charlie Peace led an incredible life, one which fully deserves to be remembered as an account of the man who had the entire nation on the lookout for him, yet managed to employ his unique chameleon-like skills again and again, fooling the authorities repeatedly.

There are certain aspects of the Charlie Peace legend which have been deliberately, but sadly, omitted from this book on the grounds that there is every possibility that they may not, in fact, be true. So popular was Peace as the subject of Victorian comic strips and penny dreadfuls, that these fascinating anecdotes are more than likely to be the work of a nineteenth century literary wit than a true account of his actions.

One such example is the comical tale of Peace escaping from an approaching policeman by dashing into the halls of a nearby grammar school where, unable to conceal himself before being spotted, the cunning little man with the limp began to perform Shakespearian soliloquies to the wide-eyed boys who entered the room in which he was hiding, pretending, as if his life depended upon it, to be a travelling actor.

Another tall tale involves the diminutive burglar disappearing up a chimney upon being discovered in the parlour of an unsuspecting gentleman, before climbing out onto the roof, black from head to toe, and making his daring getaway across the high rooftops.

Such stories, although probably fabricated, serve to transform the story of Charlie Peace into the legend of Charlie Peace. Yet time has not been kind to the memory of this extraordinary character. Mention the name of Charlie Peace to anyone outside the Sheffield boundaries, and more often than not you will be greeted by a sea of blank expressions.

Much of the Victorian fascination with the life and crimes of this hobbling burglar was to fall by the wayside during the emergence of another Victorian scoundrel, a criminal who was never identified, yet held an entire city in the palm of his blood-stained hand. It was Jack the Ripper who replaced Peace on the front covers of the gaudy crime journals, and who would rob the Yorkshireman of the limelight for future generations.

However, it is important to remember that, despite his obvious flaws, Peace was a criminal genius. His talent for disguise and ability to enter a home unnoticed before leaving without a trace is, and always will be, second to none. His skills were the talk of the town during his illicit sprees, and the bane of every policeman who was called to investigate.

Due to the sheer amount of his relatively short life being spent behind bars, many would be forgiven for thinking that Peace was a fairly ordinary burglar until later in his career; however, it should be remembered that for every time he was arrested and imprisoned there were many, many occasions where he had made good his getaway and returned home with his haul.

This is not to say that a burglar should be admired. Many of us will have been victim to such a crime and so are only too aware of the distress and shock caused by such an occurrence. However, as seen in regard to the Jack the Ripper legend, we will always be fascinated by the leading characters in true crimes, especially when the subject of such a study is as notable as Charlie Peace.

A man who can become another man at the drop of a hat deserves to be remembered, even when the need for clever disguises rises in the aftermath of terrible crimes. As a species, we will always appreciate ingenuity, even when it is accompanied by violence and wrongdoing; it is just the nature of humanity.

But it is equally important to remember the victims of such a man.

EPILOGUE

The lives of Nicholas Cock and Arthur Dyson should be remembered, as should the terrible fate which almost took the life of the innocent William Habron. These were men in their own right, and should be remembered as such, rather than as human footnotes to a wider story.

We should also spare a thought for the victims who suffered indirectly at the hands of Peace - the children who grew up without a father, and the woman who stuck by her husband through thick and thin, only to be relegated to nothing more than a housekeeper, owing to the base behaviour of her villainous husband.

Although completely aware of her husband's bad character at the outset of their relationship, Hannah Peace suffered more than most. By the time her husband met his end at the hands of Mr Marwood she had endured hardship, negligence, humiliation, prosecution, and several beatings at the hands of the man to whom she devoted her life.

As the lives of his wife and children disappeared from the history books at the exact moment the trapdoor opened and Peace dangled from the end of a rope, we can only hope that some degree of fortune was cast upon them in later years. If anyone was to celebrate the death of Charlie Peace, it should have been Hannah, Jane and Willie; they deserved a far better life than the one handed down to them.

Yet, despite the obvious indelible stains on his character, it is important that Charles Frederick Peace lives on in the legends of the past. Literature needs leading characters, especially ones who lived and breathed on the same streets upon which we walk today. The past is a valuable asset, one from which we still learn and benefit.

Therefore, it would seem that the way to *feel* about Charlie Peace is not to celebrate his terrible crimes, but to remember his extraordinary life. The ghosts of the past exist in ink and paper so that they may not be repeated in flesh and blood.

Ben W. Johnson

Index

Adamson, Mrs, 88-9, 91-2,
America, 129
Angel Court, 16, 21
Armley Gaol, 134, 136, 138, 150
Askern, Thomas, 134-36
Attercliffe, 42
Bailey, Mr, 89
Banner Cross, 66-7, 69, 71, 74-5,
  79, 81, 102, 114-15, 122, 125,
  127, 130, 132, 143
Banner Cross Hotel, the, 67, 74,
  79, 81, 132,
Banner Cross Terrace, 69, 71
Barnsley, 15
Bath, 86
Beanland, Constable, 58-60
Benson, Mr John, 78
Bent, Police Superintendent, 60-2
Beverley, 85, 130
Billingsgate Street, 98
Blackheath, 102-03, 105, 111,
Bolsover, Mr, 97, 128,
Boulsover, Thomas, 9
Bradbury, Inspector, 75-6, 82
Brassington, Charles, 67-8, 79-
  80, 132,
Brion, Henry Fersey, 100, 107-
  108, 138-9
Britannia Road, 45, 127
Camberwell, 96
Campbell-Foster, Mr, 129
Castle, Sheffield, 8-10

Chatham, 36
Chesterfield, 41
Chorlton-cum-Hardy, 58
Clegg, W.H., 125-26
Cleveland, Ohio, 43, 47, 81
Cock, Constable Nicholas, 56-63,
  103, 139-40, 144, 157
Colgrave, Mrs Sarah, 67, 78-80,
  128-29
Crookes, 83, 130, 155
Darnall, 42-3, 45, 48, 53, 111,
  120-21, 127, 139, 142, 148
Deakin, Mr, 55, 61, 63
Derby, 13, 87
Dill, Doctor, 60
Don Valley, 10-11
Dyson, Arthur, 43-51, 68-9, 72-6,
  80, 82, 90, 96, 103, 115, 124,
  127, 132, 142-44, 157
Dyson, Kate, 43-4, 46-52, 66-72,
  76-8, 80-3, 117, 127-29, 131-33,
  137, 143-44
East Terrace, 98, 108
Ecclesall Church, 76
Ecclesall Road, 66
Electoral Reform Act, 12
Endcliffe Woods, 83
Evelina Road, 98
Gibraltar, 36
Gratrix, John, 59
Gray, Susan, 88-92, 95-102, 107,
  109, 137, 148-49,

INDEX

Greer, James, 24

Greer, John, 24

Gregory, John, 69, 78-9, 128

Habron, Frank, 55, 58, 61, 62, 140

Habron, John, 55, 58, 61, 63, 140

Habron, William, 55-8, 60-3, 139-41, 157

Haines, Willie, 30, 33, 37-8, 97, 108, 120, 157

Hallam, Doctor, 122

Hawkins, Mr Justice, 112-13

Hazel Street, 108

Horry, William Frederick, 146

House of Commons, 12-13

Hull, 24, 53-4, 65, 77, 85, 90-2, 96-7, 140

Huntsman, Benjamin, 9

Jack the Ripper, 156

Jemmy, One-armed, 88

Johnson, John Henry, 136

King's Cross, 86, 115

Kiveton Park, 119-22

Lambeth, 94-5

Lancashire, 54, 60

Leeds, 13, 41, 134-36

Leeds Assizes, 127, 129, 134

Lindley, Mr Justice, 63

Littlewood, Mr, 139, 141-42, 144

Liverpool, 13, 77

Lockwood, Mr, 129, 132-33

London, 9, 17, 93-8, 100-102, 108-11, 115-16, 120, 123, 125-26, 129-30, 132, 139, 147

Lopes, Mr Justice, 129-31, 133, 137

Madame Tussauds, 7

Manchester, 12-3, 29, 41, 54, 62-3, 65-6, 68, 77, 129, 140,

Manchester Assizes, 140

Marsh, the, 87-92, 109

Marwood, William, 146-47, 149-54, 157

Masborough, 85,

Massey, John, 59-60

Midland Railway, 65

Millbank, 36

Millsand Rolling Mill, 20

Myers, Joseph, 135

Neil, Mr, 27

Newgate Gaol, 106-8, 111, 128, 130, 138

Newman, Reverend, 68-9

Nottingham, 41, 87-8, 91, 109-10, 114, 148

Old Trafford, 62

Oxford, 86-7

Parliament, 12, 141

Peace, Daniel, 18, 22 24, 148-49

Peace, Hannah, 30, 33, 37-40, 45, 49-50, 54, 90, 97-8, 101, 110, 114, 150, 157

Peace, Jane, 16, 18, 20, 22, 24, 49-50, 84, 96

Peace, Jane Jr, 30, 33, 37, 38, 96-7, 108, 157

Peace, John, 15-18, 20,

Peace, John Charles, 31-2, 36

Peace, John Jr, 18

Peace, Mary Ann, 18, 24, 26-7, 29, 40

Peckham, 98-9, 107, 109-10

Pentonville Prison, 115, 117, 125
Pollard, Mr, 126-27
Robinson, Constable, 103-04, 112
Rotherham, 10, 15, 30, 41, 82, 85, 130, 135,
Royal Oak Pub, the, 55-8
Sargisson, James, 135
Sheffield, 7-13, 15-6, 19-20, 24-6, 36, 41-5, 51, 64-6, 74-6, 84-5, 91, 96, 101, 108, 111, 114-17, 121-32, 139-40, 147-49, 154-56
Sheffield and Rotherham Independent, 51, 82, 154
Spring Street, 84, 130
Steelworks, 10, 15
Strangeways, 30
Tommy, 96, 98, 100, 102
United States of America, 127

Wakefield, 32, 139
Ward, Constable, 81
Ward, John, 107-09, 112, 120, 123, 129, 138
Welby, Mr, 125
West Bar, 84
Westminster, 12, 95
Whalley Range, 54-5, 59, 63, 103, 139-40
Whyman, Charles, 80
Wicker, the, 131
Wightman, Mr, 74, 75, 80
Williams, Montagu, 112-3
Wombwell, George, 17, 18
Worksop, 119
Yorkshire, 7-11, 29, 54, 81, 85-6, 91, 101, 109, 118, 129, 147